Diseases and Disorders

Asthma

Titles in the Diseases and Disorders series include:

Diseases and Disorders

Asthma

by Barbara Sheen

LUCENT BOOKS®

THOMSON
™
GALE

San Diego • Detroit • New York • San Francisco • Cleveland
New Haven, Conn. • Waterville, Maine • London • Munich

THOMSON

✶

™

GALE

LIBRARY OF CONGRESS CATALOGING-IN-PUBLICATION DATA

Sheen, Barbara.
    Asthma / by Barbara Sheen.
v. cm. — (Diseases and disorders)
Includes bibliographical references and index.
Summary: The history, diagnosis, treatment of, increases in, and living with asthma.
    ISBN 1-59018-235-9
    1. Asthma—Juvenile literature. [1. Asthma. 2. Diseases.] I. Title. II. Diseases and disorders series
    RC591 .S534 2003
    616.2'38—dc21

                                                        2002007294

Printed in the United States of America

Table of Contents

"The Most Difficult Puzzles Ever Devised"

CHARLES BEST, ONE of the pioneers in the search for a cure for diabetes, once explained what it is about medical research that intrigued him so. "It's not just the gratification of knowing one is helping people," he confided, "although that probably is a more heroic and selfless motivation. Those feelings may enter in, but truly, what I find best is the feeling of going toe to toe with nature, of trying to solve the most difficult puzzles ever devised. The answers are there somewhere, those keys that will solve the puzzle and make the patient well. But how will those keys be found?"

Since the dawn of civilization, nothing has so puzzled people—and often frightened them, as well—as the onset of illness in a body or mind that had seemed healthy before. A seizure, the inability of a heart to pump, the sudden deterioration of muscle tone in a small child—being unable to reverse such conditions or even to understand why they occur was unspeakably frustrating to healers. Even before there were names for such conditions, even before they were understood at all, each was a reminder of how complex the human body was, and how vulnerable.

While our grappling with understanding diseases has been frustrating at times, it has also provided some of humankind's most heroic accomplishments. Alexander Fleming's accidental discovery in 1928 of a mold that could be turned into penicillin has resulted in the saving of untold millions of lives. The isolation of the enzyme insulin has reversed what was once a death sentence for anyone with diabetes. There have been great strides in combating conditions for which there is not yet a cure, too. Medicines can help AIDS patients live longer, diagnostic tools such as mammography and ultrasounds can help doctors find tumors while they are treatable, and laser surgery techniques have made the most intricate, minute operations routine.

This "toe-to-toe" competition with diseases and disorders is even more remarkable when seen in a historical continuum. An astonishing amount of progress has been made in a very short time. Just two hundred years ago, the existence of germs as a cause of some diseases was unknown. In fact, it was less than 150 years ago that a British surgeon named Joseph Lister had difficulty persuading his fellow doctors that washing their hands before delivering a baby might increase the chances of a healthy delivery (especially if they had just attended to a diseased patient)!

Each book in Lucent's *Diseases and Disorders* series explores a disease or disorder and the knowledge that has been accumulated (or discarded) by doctors through the years. Each book also examines the tools used for pinpointing a diagnosis, as well as the various means that are used to treat or cure a disease. Finally, new ideas are presented—techniques or medicines that may be on the horizon.

Frustration and disappointment are still part of medicine, for not every disease or condition can be cured or prevented. But the limitations of knowledge are being pushed outward constantly; the "most difficult puzzles ever devised" are finding challengers every day.

A Growing Epidemic

DANIEL* WAS DIAGNOSED with asthma when he was four years old. He often woke up during the night coughing and gasping for air. Whenever he played outside, he became easily winded and had difficulty catching his breath. Once after playing in the snow, he had so much trouble breathing that he was rushed to the hospital. That's when Daniel and his family learned that he was one of 17 million Americans afflicted with asthma. Of these, more than one-quarter are children.

Asthma is a disorder that affects a person's ability to breathe. It is the most common chronic disorder found in American children and the third most common chronic disease in adults. Moreover, the number of asthma cases is growing rapidly. In the last two decades, the number of asthma cases in the United States increased by more than 60 percent and, in the same time period, asthma deaths tripled. Every day, approximately fourteen Americans die of asthma, as compared to five Americans per day twenty years ago.

This problem is not limited to the United States. Asthma rates have been increasing throughout the world. A parent of an asthmatic in Australia talks about the epidemic:

> In the area around [the city of] Melbourne where we live asthma is incredibly common now. I can't think of any of our friends where there isn't at least one member of the family

---

**Author's note: All last names have been omitted to protect the interviewees' privacy.*

with asthma, and often it's both children. If you go to a school sports day, you'll see the teachers going along the line of kids saying, "Have you taken your asthma medication?" It's so much a part of everyday life now.[1]

Because the incidence of asthma is so widespread and has such a tremendous impact on society, government organizations throughout the world, including the U.S. Department of Health and Human Services, have instituted programs to raise public awareness about asthma. Doctors and scientists hope that these programs will help lessen the burden that asthma places on the health care system. Currently, more than 1.8 million Americans visit emergency rooms every year because of

Those who suffer from severe asthma attacks are often rushed to the hospital for treatment.

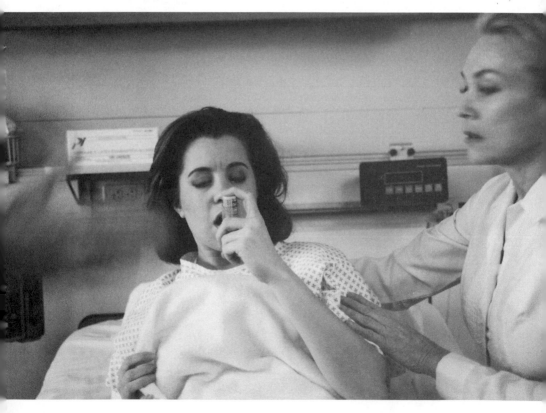

asthma complications. Of these people, more than a half-million are hospitalized. Asthma-related health care costs are estimated to be more than $6 billion a year.

Health care costs are not the only burden asthma places on society. Asthma causes workers to miss 9 million workdays per year, making it the fourth leading cause of work loss in America. So many missed days costs society $1 billion per year.

The effect on children is even more severe. Asthma is the leading cause of school absences. American children miss more than 10 million school days each year as a result of asthma, which is about eleven days per child. Now a young adult, Daniel recalls how asthma affected his school attendance: "I missed a lot of school when I was a kid. We lived in New York then, and cold weather and wind really strained my lungs. I had asthma attacks all winter long. It's amazing that I learned to read, because I probably missed more of first grade than I attended."[2]

Because asthma's impact is so far reaching, it is important that people understand the disorder. By learning about what causes

The effects of asthma are more severe in children than in adults.

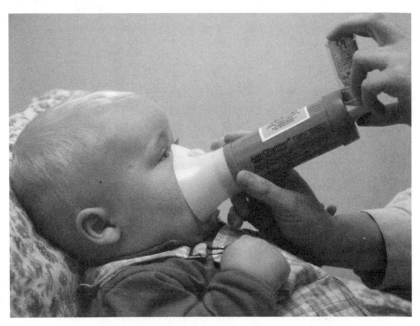

asthma, how to treat it, and the challenges it presents, friends and family members will gain a better understanding of how to provide asthma sufferers with appropriate support. Patients and their families will be able to make better choices about their treatment and learn ways to manage and control their disorder.

At twenty, Daniel has learned quite a bit about asthma and how to manage it. Today, he is a successful college student who rarely misses classes because of asthma. Like many other people with asthma, he has learned how to control the disorder. "It seems like I've had asthma all my life," he explains. "But hey, life's not perfect, and there's a lot worse things than asthma. Besides, I've learned how to deal with it. I'm planning on graduating in a couple of years, and after that, who knows? Whatever I decide to do, asthma is not going to stop me."[3]

Chapter 1

What Is Asthma?

A STHMA IS A disorder of the respiratory system that affects a person's lungs and ability to breathe. When asthma strikes, the airways become blocked, making breathing difficult. No one knows exactly what causes asthma or why some people develop it.

Asthma is a chronic disorder. Once a person develops it, there is no cure. People with asthma may have symptoms that come and go, but the disorder itself affects them for life. One asthma sufferer explains what this means: "When I was a little girl I asked my doctors if I would ever be well, able to run and play, [and] they told me I had a serious medical problem. 'You were born with asthma and it will always be with you. Just get used to it,' they said."[4]

What Type of Disorder Is Asthma?

Asthma is primarily an allergic disorder in which the lungs respond inappropriately to harmless substances in the environment known as allergens. This occurs when the immune system, which protects the body from foreign invaders like bacteria or viruses, mistakes allergens (such as dust, pollen, animal hair, or mold) for foreign invaders and sends white blood cells to attack and destroy them. When the white blood cells come in contact with allergens, they produce chemicals known as histamines, which irritate the lungs and cause breathing problems.

Although not every asthma patient suffers from allergies, 90 percent of children with asthma and more than 70 percent of adults with asthma do. Even though scientists do not know what causes asthma in the rest of the population or whether allergies actually cause asthma, many scientists believe there is a definite link between the two. They theorize that the overproduction of histamines and the resulting irritation weakens the lungs of people with asthma, making them more susceptible to asthma attacks. Asthma expert Dr. Betty B. Wray describes how allergies affect Malcolm, one of her patients: "He has an intense allergic reaction to cats and dogs. Just being in the same room where a pet has been can make Malcolm's throat close up. A minute later he's coughing up mucus, and sometimes his chest constricts [tightens up], and an asthma attack threatens."[5]

How Asthma Affects the Lungs

All people with asthma, regardless of its cause, experience breathing problems when their lungs overreact to things in the environment. Normally, when a person breathes, oxygen and carbon dioxide travel in and out of the body through a roadlike network known as the airways. Oxygen is inhaled through the

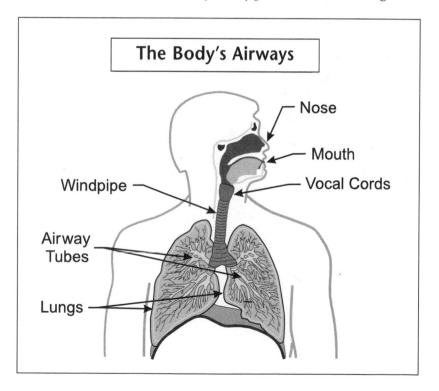

The Body's Airways

Nose

Mouth

Vocal Cords

Windpipe

Airway Tubes

Lungs

nose or mouth and passes through a long hollow tube called the windpipe. The windpipe branches off into two smaller tubes called bronchi that connect to the lungs. The lungs contain smaller tubes called bronchioles, and in these tubes oxygen is exchanged for carbon dioxide. If an irritant such as smoke or dust is inhaled, the lining of the airways becomes swollen or inflamed, and mucus, a thick, sticky substance used to trap irritants, is secreted. This response, which is the immune system's way of protecting the lungs, causes most people to cough, expelling the irritant and stopping the inflammatory process.

When people with asthma inhale an irritant, however, these same defenses overreact instead of protecting the lungs. This results in an obstruction of the airways. Unchecked inflammation causes the swollen airways to narrow, and the production of excess mucus forms gooey plugs that clog up the narrow airways. At the same time, the smooth muscles that surround the windpipe and bronchi tighten up, squeezing the airways. The swelling, mucus plugs, and constricting muscles make it difficult for air to move in or out of the lungs.

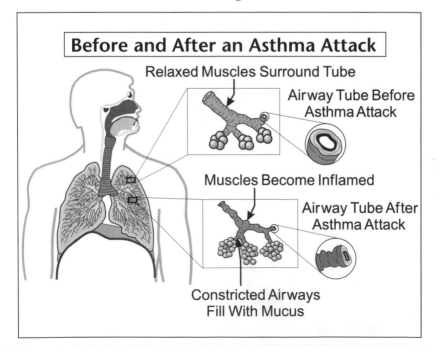

Before and After an Asthma Attack

Relaxed Muscles Surround Tube

Airway Tube Before Asthma Attack

Muscles Become Inflamed

Airway Tube After Asthma Attack

Constricted Airways Fill With Mucus

The lungs of people with asthma react this way because they are hyperreactive. This means that they overreact to substances in the airways that do not normally trouble other people. According to asthma expert Dr. Jonathan Brostoff, "The problem is the airways are over-sensitive or hyper-reactive: in other words, they narrow at the smallest provocation."[6]

An Asthma Attack

When this hyperreaction gets out of control, the result is an asthma attack, or asthma episode. During an asthma attack, the airways become so obstructed that it takes more and more effort to force air through them. A whistling sound called wheezing may occur as the patient tries to force air through the blocked airways. Carbon dioxide, a waste product that can be poisonous to the body if it is not eliminated, builds up. The more carbon dioxide there is in the body, the more urgent the need to breathe. At the same time, oxygen, which is needed for life, is unable to enter the body. Since very little air can get in or out during an asthma attack, patients often feel like they are suffocating. Consequently, an asthma attack can be quite frightening.

Asthma attacks can be mild, moderate, or severe, depending on how badly the airways are blocked. Fortunately, mild and moderate attacks are the most common. Some attacks can come on quickly, while other attacks build up over several days.

During an attack, people with asthma report feeling tightness around their chest (caused by a combination of their muscles constricting and the buildup of carbon dioxide), an icy sensation in their lungs (caused by the lack of air), and difficulty breathing. The struggle to breathe can be exhausting, and many patients are overcome with fatigue after an attack. One patient describes a typical attack for him:

> I can't catch my breath. It's the same way you might feel after running a race, but I may just be sitting and watching TV when it happens and it doesn't let up. My throat and chest start to clinch up and hurt. It's like someone tightly cinched a belt around my chest. When I breathe, there's a cold tingly

feeling. I can't talk. My breaths are shallow. Since my throat and chest are closing up, I make a hissing sound that everyone calls wheezing. If the attack is bad, it's almost like drowning. After a while my whole chest aches and I'm really tired. When I first started having attacks it scared me a lot. I thought I was going to suffocate. But it doesn't scare me now because I'm used to it.[7]

Attack Triggers

Certain things cause the airways of asthmatics to overreact. These are called asthma triggers. Triggers can be physical or emotional. Allergens, pollution, weather extremes, respiratory infections, chemicals found in medicine, exercise, excitement, and stress are all examples of asthma triggers.

Common allergens such as pollen, dust, and animal hair often cause a hyperreactive response when asthma patients inhale them. Substances found in polluted air such as smog, smoke, diesel fuel, and sulfur dioxide, a chemical produced by some factories, also contain irritants that may provoke an asthma attack. When vehicles burn diesel fuel, for example, tiny particles are sent into the air that irritate the sensitive lungs of people with asthma. In fact, a study in England found that when diesel fuel levels rise, so do the number of asthma attacks.

Extreme weather conditions are another trigger that frequently causes the airways of asthmatics to tighten. Cold weather, for example, can be a particular concern. When cold air hits anyone's face, nerves in the skin direct the muscles around the airways to contract, causing people to breathe harder. In most people, this response is temporary, but in people with asthma, it can set off an attack. Other weather conditions such as humidity and electricity in the air during thunderstorms are also common triggers. During these conditions, trees and plants release higher than normal levels of pollen. This increase in pollen causes allergic reactions that often result in more asthma attacks. A study in London found that, during a severe thunderstorm in 1994, hospital admissions for asthma attacks increased by more than 1,000

Upon inhalation, ragweed (above) can be an asthma trigger. Weather conditions may cause plants to release more pollen (right).

percent. According to an emergency room nurse, "The hospitals here gear up now if they know there's been a high pollen load and a thunderstorm is on the way, because they know they'll have a great influx of asthma sufferers once the storm breaks."[8]

Colds, chest infections, and chemicals in some medications can also trigger asthma attacks. The immune systems of some people with asthma overreact to certain viruses and to some chemicals in medicine by becoming swollen and inflamed. This leads to asthma attacks. One woman explains how chemicals in eyedrops triggered her asthma:

> I used these drops twice a day. It was just after that my asthma started playing up, only it never dawned on me that it had anything to do with the drops. You wouldn't think something going into your eyes could affect your chest would you? I went out shopping with two of my friends, and I had to keep stopping to get my breath. My chest was really hurting. I went back to the doctor. She looked at my notes and said "Oh dear, you shouldn't really have been given those." . . . As soon as I stopped using the drops I began feeling better.[9]

Exercise, which dries out moisture in the lungs and makes everyone breathe faster, also triggers attacks in some asthma pa-

Playing in cold weather can often trigger an asthma attack.

tients. Moisture in the lungs, which is normally replaced when people catch their breath, cannot be replaced in some asthmatics. The loss of moisture forces the muscles around the airways to contract, making it difficult to breathe. Experts estimate that almost 90 percent of all asthma patients sometimes experience exercise as an asthma trigger. As one asthma patient explains, "Whenever I do certain types of aerobic exercise, where I am running or jumping, or I'm really pushing my limits, my chest starts to hurt and I know that if I don't stop I'll have an asthma attack. Running hard and playing basketball are definite triggers. I can't do either. If I do, I run out of air. My lungs feel like they're straining to work, and my body panics. It's similar to trying to suck air through a bent straw, or at least that's what it feels like."[10]

Stress and excitement can also trigger asthma attacks. Crying or laughing causes people to breathe more forcefully, which makes the airways contract. Stress can also lead to a gradual tightening of the airways. Thus, many people report having an asthma attack after a traumatic event such as a death in the family. According to one asthma sufferer,

> When my dad died, my asthma flared up. I read that extreme emotions could trigger asthma, but it never happened to me before. We were very close, and I was extremely upset. I don't know if all the crying had anything to do with it. But from the moment I heard that he was dead until the day we buried him, I had one attack after another. It was like my whole body was grieving for him. Every part of me, including my lungs, was stressed and out of control.[11]

Specific triggers that affect people with asthma vary from person to person. Some people may have only one trigger, whereas others may respond to a number of different triggers individually or in combination. A teacher explains how the combination of cold air and exercise triggers asthma symptoms in one of her students: "It never fails. Every time she goes outside and runs around and plays in the cold, she comes in wheezing and gasping for air, looking for her inhaler. She can run around and play on warm sunny days without any problem, and she can go outside and sit quietly on cold days without needing her inhaler, but whenever she exercises in the cold air she always has breathing problems."[12]

People at Risk

Although there is no way of predicting who will get asthma and no way to prevent it, certain people do appear to be at greater risk. Among those at risk are people with particular professions, such as firefighters, bakers, hairdressers, painters, and certain factory workers who inhale harmful substances on the job. Firefighters, for example, are exposed to smoke and dozens of different irritants, such as smoldering wood chips, burning paper and rubber, and soot and dust on a daily basis. Over time, all of these irritants can weaken and irritate firefighters' airways, often resulting in the development of asthma.

Likewise, bakers inhale flour dust and hairdressers inhale several different chemicals found in different hair preparations that can act as allergens and irritants. The longer a person is exposed to an allergen, the more severe his or her allergic reaction. Thus, after years of constant exposure, many bakers and hairdressers develop asthma. Dr. Betty B. Wray discusses the case of Lydia, a baker with the beginnings of asthma:

> Lydia is twenty-four years old and works in a bakery. For the past several weeks, she's been coughing and wheezing at work, and it doesn't stop until just before bedtime. The problem seems to clear up on weekends, but during the workweek, she feels as though she's continually trying to catch her breath. Lydia used to go to the gym after work, but since the shortness of breath started, she just doesn't feel able to exercise. Once, when she was running on the treadmill, she felt like she was suffocating, and she had to stop and cough for several minutes before she could gain breath normally.[13]

Two other high-risk groups are painters, especially those who use spray paints, and factory workers in plants that deal with plastics, rubber, and certain chemicals. These two groups are exposed to chemicals called isocyanates that are extremely irritating to the lungs. For this reason, they often wear special masks to minimize isocyanate contact with their lungs. Unfortunately, because isocyanates are so irritating to the lungs, even a slight exposure can cause problems. Therefore, even when such precautions are taken, many people still develop asthma.

People who have family members with asthma are also considered at higher risk, since asthma appears to run in families. As a result, many experts think that the susceptibility to develop asthma is inherited. Studies have shown that the more close relatives with asthma a person has, the greater that person's chances of developing the disorder. According to one study, children in families in which neither parent has asthma have only a 6 percent chance of developing the disorder. If one parent has asthma, children's chances of developing it rise to 28 percent, and if both parents have asthma, the chances rise to more than 63 percent. Another study that looked at identical twins found that

People who work with chemicals and other asthma triggers use masks to prevent inhalation of the harmful substances.

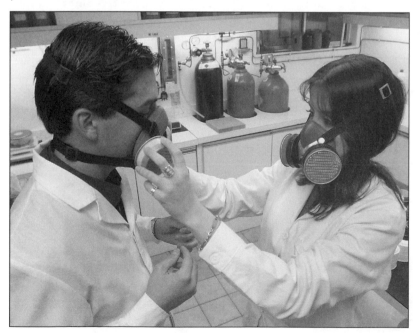

when one twin was afflicted with asthma, 70 percent of the other twins had it too. An identical twin talks about this phenomenon: "Asthma runs in my family, like freckles or curly hair do in other families. Both my brother [his identical twin] and I have asthma. I've had it since I was a baby. My brother didn't develop it until he was five, but we both have pretty severe cases now. Our little brother has asthma too, and so does our mom, but their asthma isn't as severe as ours."[14]

African Americans are another high-risk group. Sixty-one out of every one thousand African Americans in the United States suffer from asthma. Even more troubling, asthma strikes African Americans more severely than it does any other group. African Americans are four times more likely to visit emergency rooms because of severe asthma attacks than other ethnic groups, and they are three times more likely to die of asthma. African American males appear to be at higher risk than females. Twenty-six percent of all African American males between the ages of fifteen and forty have asthma. An African American teenager describes his experience: "All the males in my family have asthma. I have it. My daddy has it. So do all my uncles and cousins. My grandaddy has it too. But my mom and my sister seem to be immune. I guess it's a male thing. When I have a son, he'll probably have it too."[15] Experts are uncertain why this group is at such risk. They hypothesize, however, that since many African Americans live in urban areas, the combination of exposure to high rates of pollution, indoor allergens, and heredity make this group particularly vulnerable.

How Many People Are Affected?

Although people in higher risk groups may be more likely to develop asthma, no one is immune to the disorder. It affects people of all races and age groups. In fact, more and more people are diagnosed with asthma every day. According to the Bureau of Health Statistics, asthma rates are skyrocketing, with the largest increase occurring in children and teenagers. Since 1995, asthma rates in this group have more than doubled. Today, about 5.5 million Americans under the age of eighteen suffer from asthma.

Since experts do not know what causes asthma, they are unable to explain why asthma rates are increasing so rapidly. However, because of the increasing levels of common asthma triggers, such as pollution and allergens in the environment, experts predict that these rates will continue to climb.

Physical Impact of Asthma

No matter who gets asthma, the disorder usually has a physical impact on the body. Repeated asthma attacks can cause permanent

A young girl uses an inhaler. The number of children and teenagers with asthma has increased significantly since 1995.

lung damage. Repeated swelling, combined with the secretion of mucus and other potent chemicals, erodes the lining of the lungs, destroying and damaging cells. The damaged cells become thick and scarred, which makes it difficult for blood and air to pass through the lungs. When this happens, people with asthma suffer from regular breathing problems. In addition, the violent coughing that often occurs during severe asthma attacks can fracture ribs, rupture blood vessels, and cause the lungs to collapse.

Frequent asthma attacks can also lead to a hunched-over, barrel-chested appearance. People with asthma repeatedly use muscles to breathe that people without asthma use only after strenuous exercise. These muscles, which surround the neck, ribs, collarbone, and breastbone, help expand the rib cage in order to allow more air to be taken in. When these muscles are used often, the lungs become permanently overinflated and the chest becomes contorted, resulting in a hunched-over, barrel-chested appearance.

Asthma can do more than damage the lungs and posture; asthma attacks can affect the whole body. When the body repeatedly gets less oxygen than it needs to function properly, every cell in the body is forced to work harder to compensate for the lack of oxygen. Over time, this can weaken the whole body and make people with asthma more susceptible to contracting other diseases.

When Asthma Threatens Lives

Although asthma can usually be controlled, severe asthma attacks can cause death. Rare, life-threatening asthma attacks are known as status asthmaticus. Status asthmaticus occurs when the airways become so constricted, inflamed, and swollen that almost no air can pass through them. This makes breathing so difficult that patients often become too exhausted to push air in and out.

When the symptoms become this extreme, medication that usually relieves an asthmatic's symptoms is ineffective. In this situation, the asthmatic is admitted to a hospital and given a shot of adrenaline, a powerful chemical that opens up breathing passages. In severe cases, this may not work. If the adrenaline shot is not successful, the patient is hooked up to an artificial breathing machine called a respirator. The respirator is attached to a tube placed down the patient's windpipe that causes the lungs to inflate and deflate automatically, allowing the person to breathe.

Experts are not sure what causes status asthmaticus, but they hypothesize that such attacks result either when patients' lungs have been weakened by prolonged exposure to an abnormally high volume of asthma triggers or, following a serious attack, when patients resume normal activities before their weakened lungs have adequate time to recuperate. According to asthma expert Dr. Joe Collier, "One of the most vulnerable times for an asthmatic is just when he or she is beginning to recover after a serious attack. They fail to recognize the severity of their disability and are prone to over-exert themselves while neglecting vital medication. I have seen such ill-judged over-confidence kill patients who were released from the hospital too soon."[16]

Experts do not conclusively know what causes life-threatening asthma. They do know, however, that millions of Americans are afflicted with this frightening and widespread disorder. And they predict that even more people will contract asthma in the future.

Chapter 2

Diagnosis and Conventional Treatment

W HEN PEOPLE EXPERIENCE problems breathing, asthma is often suspected. However, diagnosing asthma can be difficult and time-consuming because asthma symptoms are as varied as the people who have them. Fortunately, once asthma has been diagnosed, drug treatment can keep symptoms under control, limit attacks, and greatly improve the lives of people with asthma.

Diagnosing Asthma

Diagnosing asthma can be tricky. Many asthma symptoms closely resemble symptoms of other ailments, which can lead to a misdiagnosis. For example, frequent coughing and wheezing, which trouble many people with asthma, are often mistaken for bacterial or viral infections of the lungs such as bronchitis, pneumonia, tuberculosis, and whooping cough. Similarly, the tightening of the chest and windpipe is sometimes mistaken for acid reflux, a digestive disorder that produces similar symptoms. Some forms of heart disease and lung cancer can also produce asthmalike symptoms. A man with asthma describes how confusing asthma symptoms can be: "I was twenty-one when I developed asthma. I didn't know it was asthma—I thought I had a problem with my lungs or my throat because I used to cough badly and produce a lot of phlegm. This cough went on for several weeks and didn't improve, so I went to my doctor and he said, 'Basically, you've got asthma.' I was really surprised."[17]

One group for whom asthma is often misdiagnosed is the elderly. Because 80 percent of asthma symptoms usually first appear before children are five years old, when people over sixty exhibit asthma symptoms, the possibility of their being afflicted with asthma is frequently overlooked. The most common

An elderly woman receives treatment after suffering from an asthma attack.

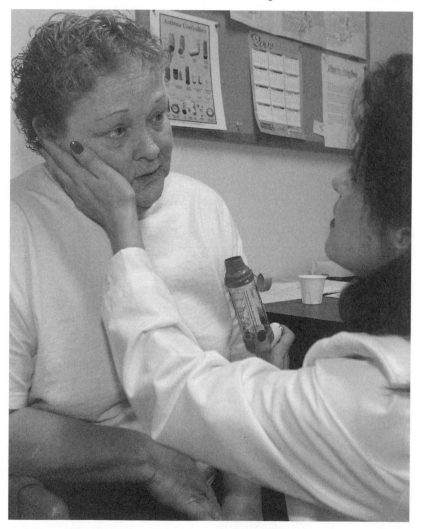

symptoms reported by asthmatics in this age group are short-ness of breath and chest tightness, which are often mistaken for heart disease or emphysema (a respiratory disease). As a result, asthma is regularly misdiagnosed and goes untreated in older people.

Young children are another group that is often misdiagnosed. Infants and toddlers cannot describe their symptoms, so parents and doctors have to rely on symptoms they can see. The first ob-vious symptom of asthma in a young child is usually wheezing. Wheezing, however, is a common symptom of many things. It can be associated with cystic fibrosis, an inherited lung disease that affects children. Wheezing can also occur when toddlers put small objects such as beads or toy parts into their nose or mouth; such objects partially block the airways and result in wheezing. Thus, many physicians suspect that wheezing toddlers have in-haled an item, have cystic fibrosis, or have another ailment rather than asthma.

Young athletes are a third group who may not be properly di-agnosed. Often, the most common symptoms found in this group are chest tightness and shortness of breath. Both, however, are fre-quently attributed as being the normal result of vigorous exercise. Consequently, members of this group may not know they are sick and, thus, do not seek medical help. When American competitors in the 1984 Summer Olympics were tested for asthma, for in-stance, seventy-seven athletes showed symptoms of the disorder. Of these, eighteen did not realize they had asthma. Another study of high-school football players in Philadelphia found that 9 per-cent suffered from undiagnosed asthma. According to Jim Rogers, the director of Sports' Asthma Research at Temple University, "There is a lot of undiagnosed asthma at all levels of athletic par-ticipation. Athletes are getting inadequate treatment, causing them to wheeze, cough and struggle for breath when exercising. Athletes are routinely screened for heart murmurs and hernias, but rarely for asthma."[18]

The problem of undiagnosed asthma in young athletes can be especially serious since the combination of lack of treatment and vigorous exercise can lead to life-threatening asthma attacks. A sports research study at Temple University, for example, reported that, between 1995 and 2000, sixty-one children and adolescents died from asthma during or after an athletic event.

Symptoms

Despite the problems with diagnosis, there are certain symptoms that indicate the presence of asthma. These include coughing, wheezing, tightening of the chest, shortness of breath, the feeling of not getting enough air, and tingling or numbness in the fingers and toes. Individual asthma symptoms rarely exist on their own. Generally, a patient has several symptoms at once. This is because inflammation, narrowed airways, and the lack of oxygen produce a number of complications. One man who suffers from asthma describes his experience:

> I had a sharp dry cough that made me sound like a barking dog, and sometimes when I was coughing my chest would start hurting. I thought it was from coughing too hard. I was short of breath too, and sometimes my fingers would kind of tickle and go numb. That was really odd, coughing and tickling fingers. . . . When I told the doctor about it, I thought he was going to say I was crazy. Instead, he explained that my fingers probably felt that way because there wasn't enough oxygen reaching them. Then he tested me for asthma.[19]

Testing

Since there is no single test that conclusively proves that a patient has asthma, when asthma is suspected, doctors administer a number of tests. Because people with asthma often have trouble taking deep breaths without coughing or wheezing, patients are first given a physical exam that focuses on the way they breathe. Doctors also look for physical signs of asthma such as hunched shoulders and a barrel chest. In addition, to rule out other diseases such as pneumonia, bronchitis, and lung cancer, chest X rays are often taken.

If asthma symptoms appear to be linked to allergies, a doctor will administer an allergy test. In an allergy test, a small

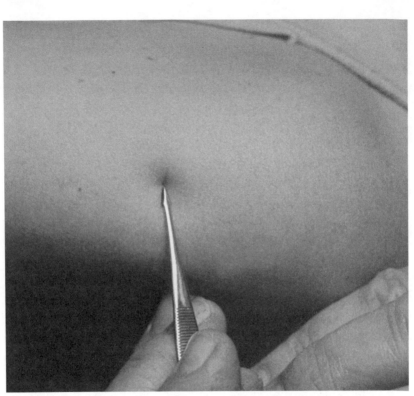

To test for allergic reactions, doctors place allergens under a patient's skin.

amount of liquid containing an allergen, such as pollen or mold, is placed under the patient's skin. If a red bump appears, it indicates an allergy. In some cases, patients may be given small amounts of an allergen to inhale. Then, doctors observe the effects on the person's airways. Since this test can cause a severe asthma attack, though, it is usually administered only in a hospital.

Finally, patients receive a lung function test, which measures how severely a person's airway is blocked. During a lung function test, patients blow into a machine called a spirometer. The spirometer is attached to a computer that records the force and volume of air that patients exhale. The results are compared to those of people without asthma in order to determine if the patient's airway is blocked. If the results are lower than 80 percent, which is normal, patients are given medication that relaxes the airways of asthmatics and then given another lung function test. This second test determines if the airways' obstruction is caused by asthma or another respiratory disorder since only asthmatics respond to the medication.

Many asthma experts consider lung function tests the most reliable way to measure how well a person's lungs are working. According to the National Heart, Lung, and Blood Institute's Guidelines for the Diagnosis and Management of Asthma, "[Lung function tests] are particularly important because subjective measures [those that require an opinion], such as patient symptom reports and physicians' physical examination findings, often don't [accurately reflect] the severity of airflow obstruction. Pulmonary [lung] function studies are essential for diagnosing asthma and for assessing the severity of asthma."[20]

Four Stages of Severity

Once a doctor diagnoses a patient's asthma, treatment with medication can begin. The goal of treatment is to control asthma symptoms, reduce the frequency and severity of asthma attacks, and relieve airway obstruction. Because severe cases of asthma require powerful medication, doctors analyze the severity of a patient's symptoms in order to prescribe an appropriate treatment. To simplify this process, the National Institutes of Health, the largest health organization in the United States, provides guidelines for the diagnosis and management of asthma. These guidelines divide asthma into four stages or levels of severity: mild intermittent, mild persistent, moderate persistent, and severe persistent.

Symptoms in each stage of severity vary. In mild intermittent asthma, symptoms generally occur less than once a week. Symptoms occur more than once a week in mild persistent asthma, making it more troublesome. In moderate persistent asthma, symptoms occur daily and interfere with many activities. Symptoms are so severe in severe persistent asthma that they occur almost continuously and limit patients' physical activities.

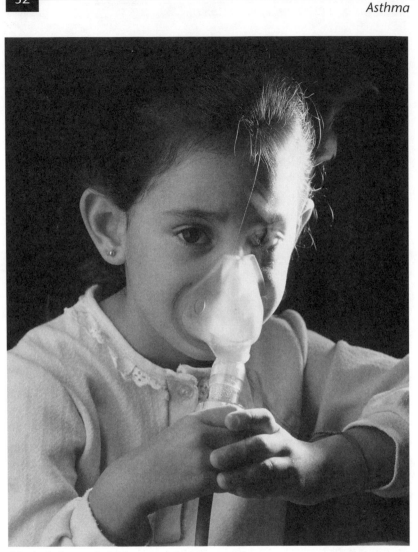

Masks help small children use inhalers properly.

Medications and Their Effects

There are a number of medications used to treat asthma, but they can be divided into two general categories: preventers, also known as long-term controllers, and short-term, quick-relief medicines, or bronchodilators. Although these medications work in different ways, the goal of both is to relax the airways of asthma sufferers.

Long-term controllers and quick-relief medicines can be taken in many forms, including pills and syrups, but the most common method is through an inhaler. An inhaler is a small hand-held instrument that contains a measured dose of medication, which is sprayed directly into the airways via the mouth. The medicine's purpose is to open up the airways and relieve asthma symptoms. There are many different types of inhalers, but the most common resemble a small spray can with a nozzle on one end, where medication mists out, and a device called a spacer on the other end, which holds the medication until patients can breathe it into their lungs.

Inhalers are simple instruments, but many young children have difficulty using them. For this reason, young children often use special inhalers that have a face mask that goes over the child's mouth.

Long-Term Controllers

No matter how they are administered, long-term controller medicines treat persistent asthma problems by interfering with the immune system. They reduce inflammation in the airways as well as the resulting coughing and wheezing. By controlling inflammation, long-term controllers lessen or prevent the occurrence of asthma attacks, but they have little effect on the airways once an attack is in progress.

There are a number of different long-term controller medicines. The most popular are corticosteroids, cromolyn, and theophylline. Corticosteroids, derived from cortisol, a chemical produced naturally by the body, are powerful drugs that suppress the immune system. They decrease swelling, reduce mucus production, and lessen the hyperresponsiveness in the airways. According to the National Heart, Lung, and Blood Institute's Guidelines for the Diagnosis and Management of Asthma, "Inhaled corticosteroid medications are the most effective means of reducing and preventing airway inflammation available today."[21]

Cromolyn is a less powerful medication than corticosteroids. As a result, it is often used to treat babies and young children who may not be able to tolerate the potent effect of cortico-steroids. In addition, since cromolyn blocks the production of histamines, it is especially effective in treating asthma patients who suffer from allergies. Finally, theophylline, one of the oldest asthma medications in use, relaxes the muscles that surround the airways and lessens inflammation.

An inhaler can be a quick way to relieve asthma attacks.

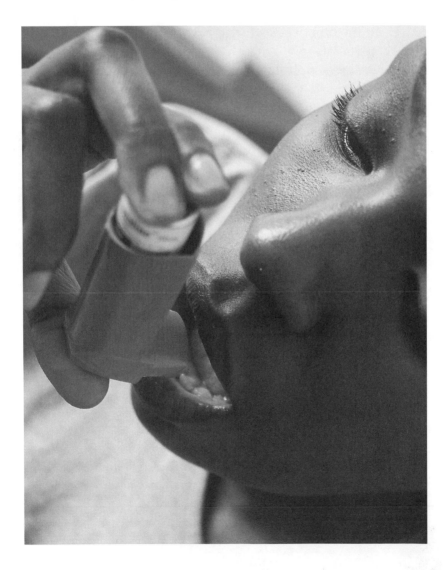

Long-term controller medications do not act immediately. They must build up in the bloodstream of asthma patients over a number of days before becoming effective. Moreover, they can control inflammation only if they are taken on a daily basis; their effects quickly wear off when treatment stops. However, when they are taken consistently, long-term controllers lower the risk of asthma attacks. When an attack does threaten, since the airways have been kept open by the use of a long-term controller, the airways do not tighten up as severely. This makes the attack less dangerous. A ten-year study in Sweden found that, when children with asthma were treated with long-term controllers, the number of children experiencing fatal asthma attacks and the number seeking emergency room treatment decreased significantly. For this reason, experts agree that treatment with long-term controllers significantly benefits people with asthma.

Quick-Relief Medication

The second type of asthma medication, bronchodilators, or quick-relief medications, are rescue drugs used to treat all four stages of asthma. Bronchodilators provide fast, temporary relief, helping stop asthma attacks both when symptoms threaten and after attacks have started. They do this by relaxing the constricted muscles that squeeze the airways during an asthma attack. Chemicals in bronchodilators attach to and stimulate cells called beta-receptors located in the small muscles surrounding the airways. Stimulating beta-receptors causes the muscles to relax and the airways to open, allowing asthmatics to breathe easier.

The most common quick-relief medicines are called beta agonists and include specific drugs such as Ventolin and Proventil. Beta agonists work like adrenaline, helping the body respond rapidly to an emergency by raising the user's heart rate and blood pressure and relaxing the airways. Since bronchodilators can save asthma patients' lives, people with asthma carry inhalers with quick-relief medicine with them at all times. According to one asthma patient, "I have an inhaler with Ventolin in each of my purses. That way, I always have one with me. Although I don't use it that often, it's there if I feel an attack coming on. Just knowing I have it makes me feel more secure. I don't have to worry about asthma attacks. It is, quite literally, a life-saver."[22]

Risks and Side Effects of Asthma Medication

Despite the benefits of asthma medications, as with any drugs, there are health risks and side effects. Among the most troubling is the problem resulting from patients using their inhalers improperly and taking an incorrect dose of medication. Using an inhaler can be difficult. Medication may be lost in the air; sprayed on the tongue, cheeks, or throat; or swallowed. When any of these things occur, patients receive about 20 percent of the inhaled drug they need, an amount that cannot adequately relieve asthma symptoms. Consequently, improper inhaler use is frequently the reason that patients have difficulty controlling their asthma symptoms.

In an effort to solve this problem, many patients take repeated doses. This can result in an overdose of medication, which can be dangerous. Moreover, some inhalers may deliver large or even double doses. In the 1980s, for example, more than one thousand asthma patients in New Zealand died from what experts believe was an overdose of a beta agonist inhaled through an inhaler that mistakenly delivered a double dose with each puff.

Overuse of certain asthma medications, such as theophylline, is especially risky. There is a small difference between an effective dose of this long-term controller and a toxic dose. A normal dose is between ten and twenty micrograms. More than twenty micrograms, however, can be toxic. The slight discrepancy is especially dangerous for children and teenagers, who may unknowingly be prescribed an adult-sized dose that is inconsistent with their smaller bodies. A father whose son died of an overdose of theophylline explains: "My son Franck died following a severe asthma attack. The doctor who ordered Franck's medication did not know it was no longer manufactured in a light dosage for children. This theophylline overdose killed my son on his tenth birthday."[23]

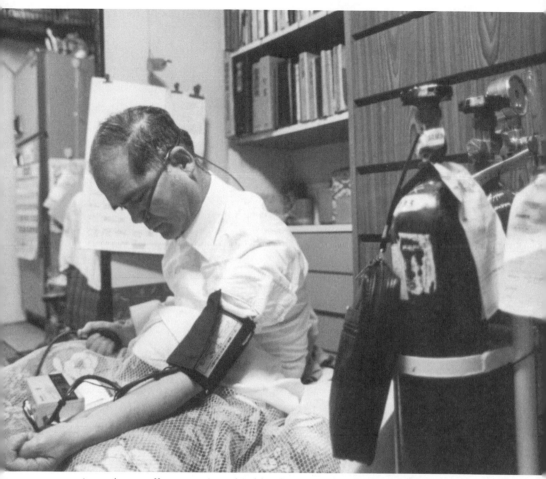

An asthma sufferer monitors his blood pressure. If asthma medicine is taken incorrectly, other health problems may arise.

In addition, asthmatics sometimes swallow medicines that are meant to be inhaled. The medicines are then absorbed by the bloodstream, resulting in a number of problems. For example, when corticosteroids are swallowed, they deplete minerals in the body such as calcium and potassium that are needed for the body to function normally. This can lead to high blood pressure, damage to the heart, and muscle weakness. Moreover, because corticosteroids suppress the immune system and mask symptoms of asthma and other illnesses, users may suffer from undetected infections such as flu or pneumonia.

Additional problems occur when corticosteroids are sprayed onto the throat rather than down the windpipe. When corticosteroids build up in a person's throat, a fungus often forms. This fungus can result in a yeast or fungal infection known as thrush, which causes a sore throat.

Health Problems Caused by Asthma Medications

Even when inhalers are used correctly, health problems can occur. Because steroids deplete minerals, inhaled steroids can cause patients' bones to become thin and fragile by depleting calcium, a mineral needed for strong, healthy bones. Researchers at Women's Hospital in Boston, for example, found a direct relationship between inhaled steroid use and loss of bone density in young women, a condition that can lead to the bone disease osteoporosis. In addition, because inhaled steroids reduce the amount of calcium needed for growth, growth may be stunted or suppressed in children who are treated with corticosteroids.

The positive effect asthma medication has on the airways can sometimes also cause problems in other parts of the body. For example, beta agonists that relax the muscles in the airways also relax the muscles in the heart, causing an asthmatic's heart to speed up and blood pressure to drop. At the same time, the adrenaline-like effect of these medications can lead to anxiety, restlessness, muscle tremors, an irregular heartbeat, and headaches.

Sometimes asthma medications are mixed with medications used to treat other diseases. This, too, can be dangerous for patients. The interaction of asthma medicines with other drugs can have a number of troubling effects. For example, when theophylline is taken at the same time as certain antibiotics, such as erythromycin, the combination can raise the potency of the theophylline to dangerous levels. Conversely, drugs such as birth control pills weaken the effect of some asthma medications. This results in increased asthma symptoms.

Possible dangerous long-term effects of asthma medication present another problem for asthmatics. Since most asthma medications are relatively new and asthma is a chronic disorder requiring treatment for a number of years, there is little information about the long-term effects of some of the newest medicines. A worried mother discusses her concerns:

> My daughter has been wheezing since she was two months old and is now seven months old. She is using a nebulizer [a special type of inhaler that converts liquid medicine into a fine mist] and gets two treatments a day of Pulmicort [a corticosteroid]. From what I understand, because she is so little it is not good for her to be on steroids for long term treatment. I can't seem to find anywhere what is considered long term treatment for steroids in infants. It is frustrating to keep giving her medicine that could potentially harm her.[24]

Exercise

Despite the risks, asthma medication can save a patient's life, and doctors believe medication is an important part of asthma treatment. However, they also suggest that patients exercise. Although exercise can trigger asthma attacks, when combined with medication it has many important benefits. Exercise strengthens the body and gives a person more energy. This is especially beneficial to people with asthma, who often suffer from fatigue caused by asthma attacks. Exercise also strengthens the heart, making it better able to deliver oxygen to the body, and the chest muscles that have been weakened by persistent asthma attacks. In addition, research has shown that exercise reduces stress, a common asthma trigger. Exercise causes the body to produce endorphins. These natural chemicals give a person a feeling of well-being that reduces stress and stress-triggered asthma attacks. And there is mounting evidence that exercise calms the immune system, allowing the body to suppress the production of chemicals that lead to inflammation.

Asthma patients are encouraged to take part in gentle forms of exercise such as ballet.

Exercise is also very important for developing good breathing habits. Many forms of exercise involve deep or controlled breathing, which can strengthen the lungs and make it easier to control asthma. And exercise can boost people's general health, which can help asthma sufferers from catching potentially dangerous infections.

Since exercise that requires prolonged running or quick bursts of energy often triggers asthma attacks, experts suggest that people with exercise-induced asthma participate in gentler forms of exercise. Such activities include walking, yoga, martial arts, weight training, ballet, cycling, or swimming. Swimming, in particular, is often recommended by asthma experts since it involves controlled breathing, strengthens the lungs, and takes place in a moist, warm environment. These factors lessen the risk of asthma attacks triggered by heavy breathing

Martial arts can be a healthy activity for asthma patients.

and cold, dry air. According to one asthma patient, "I used to have lots of attacks. Then I started swimming. I heard that it would be good for my lungs. It's great. My whole body is stronger, and I can breathe a whole lot easier. I don't get as many attacks now, either."[25]

Although asthma can be difficult to diagnose, with proper treatment, symptoms can be controlled and attacks often prevented, greatly improving the lives of people with asthma. One patient explains, "I've got asthma and both my children have it. Henry [the patient's son] is the worst. I don't feel any qualms about asthma drugs. My children have the choice of having really sickly lives dominated by asthma or of taking these drugs and running around. I sometimes stand by the playground and see Henry running like the wind, and I think that's absolutely wonderful."[26]

Chapter 3

Alternative and Complementary Treatment Strategies

I N AN EFFORT to improve their general health and the quality of their life, and to reduce their dependence on asthma medications, many people with asthma combine alternative treatments with conventional medication. This combination often helps asthma patients reduce both the frequency and amount of medication they take. It also helps them feel better.

When Patients Turn to Other Treatments

Since asthma medicines can have side effects and health risks, and since there is limited knowledge about the long-term effects of the newest asthma medications, many asthmatics explore alternative treatments in an attempt to better control their symptoms. In fact, the use of alternative treatments has grown widely among asthma patients in the last twenty years, with many reporting positive results. One young man with asthma explains why he sought alternative treatment:

> I was taking high doses of steroid medication every day and I still had to use my reliever [inhaler] when an attack threatened. That seemed to be happening more and more often. I couldn't even go to sleep without my inhaler under

my pillow. It was too much. The thought of having a life-ong dependency on steroids really scared me. I'm still a young guy, and there's no predicting what the long-term effect will be. Even my doctor doesn't know. I know I have to control the asthma, but I was feeling like it was starting to control me. That's when I decided to look into some different treatments. I don't want to stop taking medicine entirely. That would be foolish. I know the inflammation has to be controlled. But I wanted to feel less dependent and more in control. I think supplementing the medicine with a natural alternative treatment has done that for me.[27]

What Are Alternative and Complementary Treatments?

An alternative treatment is a treatment or therapy that is not widely accepted by the traditional medical community in the United States. Some forms of alternative treatments, such as acupuncture, meditation, and yoga, have been widely studied, while others have not. Regardless, unlike conventional treatments, which are subjected to rigorous testing by the Federal Drug Administration, a government agency that sets standards and regulations for the safe use of drugs, alternative treatments are not regulated by the U.S. government. Thus, they generally undergo limited testing and use anecdotal evidence taken from a few users to prove the treatment's effectiveness. Anecdotal evidence, however, often lacks enough information to show clearly whether a treatment is safe or not. This can make use of alternative treatments risky.

Despite the lack of regulation and testing, however, many doctors do believe that several alternative treatments are beneficial and that when they are combined with conventional drug treatments, in a method known as complementary treatment, they can be effective in treating asthma. Doctors suggest complementary treatment because it can reduce inflammation, open airways, lower stress, improve breathing, and give patients more control over their asthma. According to a doctor who

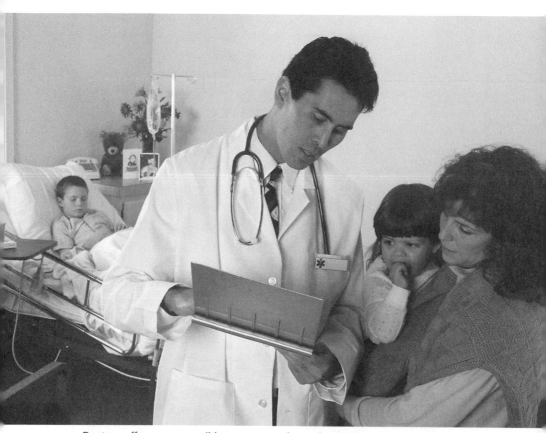

Doctors offer many possible treatments for asthma. However, patients sometimes seek out alternative treatment methods.

treats many asthmatics, "I think modern asthma drugs are amazingly good. But I wouldn't claim we [doctors who use conventional treatments] have all the answers. I've seen some patients improve dramatically when they try alternative therapy. Sometimes I can explain it, because they were anxious about their asthma before, and it calmed them down, but sometimes it's a mystery why it worked."[28]

Staying Calm Under Stress

The most widely used and accepted alternative treatments for asthma can be grouped into three categories: treatments that help patients stay calm under stress, treatments that improve breathing, and treatments that loosen chest muscles and strengthen the rib cage. Of these, treatments that help patients stay calm under stress are the most popular. One reason calming treatments are so popular is that they can save lives. Since feelings of panic often accompany an asthma attack and can exacerbate breathing problems, making an attack more severe, calming treatments can help patients retain self-control and lessen feelings of panic. Meditation, hypnotherapy, and aromatherapy are the most popular alternative treatments that help patients stay calm under stress.

In meditation, patients use concentration techniques, such as silently repeating a word or a chant, to clear the mind in order to relax the body and relieve stress. Research shows that levels of certain chemicals such as adrenaline, which the body produces as a response to stress, decrease during meditation sessions. These levels remain lowered when patients practice meditation often, thus reducing the levels of stress and anxiety that can trigger asthma attacks. Moreover, this ability to lower stress levels can help patients stay calm during an asthma attack, which can, in turn, lessen the attack's severity.

Although experts are unsure why meditation changes chemical levels in the body, the results are so impressive that many doctors as well as patients endorse using meditation as a way to control asthma. A patient discusses her experience: "I didn't start meditating because of asthma. I started because I worry a lot and I thought it would be a good way to learn to deal with my anxieties. Now I feel more in command of everything in my life, including my asthma. I'm not as anxious about my asthma, and surprisingly, I don't have as many attacks. I guess there really is a mind-body connection."[29]

Hypnotherapy is another popular method that asthmatics use to control stress. In hypnotherapy, professionals called hypnotherapists help patients enter a state of deep relaxation, known as a trance, in which the mind is more open to suggestion. While the patient is in the trance state, the hypnotherapist gives him or her suggestions that help the body relax and heal itself. Hypnotherapy is based on the theory that the mind can help the body to heal. As a result of the growing evidence of hypnotherapy's

Hypnosis can help some asthma patients control attack symptoms.

effectiveness, the College of Physicians and Surgeons at Columbia University currently offers a program on hypnosis for medical students and doctors.

Studies have shown that hypnosis can help people with asthma control asthma symptoms and improve lung capacity. This occurs because hypnotic suggestions, which promote relaxation and deep breathing, continue to affect patients long after the hypnotic trance is over. According to hypnotherapist Margaret Hutchby, "Asthma is a condition which is affected by stress and often a vicious cycle can develop with asthma symptoms creating stress which in turn leads to more asthma symptoms. Using direct suggestions aimed at improving lung capacity and teaching clients techniques to both relieve the symptoms of asthma and to reduce stress, hypnosis can help asthmatics."[30]

Aromatherapy is another treatment that people with asthma find effective in relieving stress. Aromatherapy is based on the theory that the sense of smell influences physical and psychological reactions. Consequently, it uses scent to improve mental and physical health and well-being.

In aromatherapy, asthma patients inhale warmed essential oils derived from plants believed to have anti-inflammatory or tranquilizing properties. Patients report that using these oils makes them feel more relaxed and less troubled by asthma symptoms. The oil is usually placed in a special electric diffuser or an aroma lamp. There, it heats up and disperses into the air as a mist. Patients then inhale the mist into the bloodstream through the lungs. The mist acts as an anti-inflammatory or a relaxant and calms the patient. "I keep a diffuser going 24-7 [all day long]," an asthma patient who uses aromatherapy explains. "I mix eucalyptus and lavender oil. The eucalyptus really clears up my lungs, and the lavender relaxes me. Since I started, I find I can breathe a whole lot easier, and I'm a whole lot more laid back too."[31]

Improving Breathing

Other alternative treatments seek to improve breathing. People with asthma often breathe rapidly and shallowly because of obstructed airways and anxiety. Shallow, rapid breathing is known as hyperventilation. When people hyperventilate, they breathe abnormally, using the upper chest rather than the diaphragm. This causes carbon dioxide and oxygen levels in the blood to fluctuate, leading to feelings of panic, dizziness, breathlessness, and disorientation. Although many asthma patients hyperventilate in an effort to get more air when an asthma attack threatens, some asthmatics breathe this way all the time. Learning to breathe slowly and deeply can help people with asthma control hyperventilation and soothe anxiety, allowing them to better cope with asthma symptoms.

Yoga, a form of exercise that originated in ancient India, is one way to improve an asthmatic's breathing. Yoga involves slow, controlled stretching. Stretching relaxes the body and loosens up muscles in the neck, back, and chest that have become stiff and tight as a result of repeated asthma attacks. Yoga breathing exercises focus on slow deep breathing, in which out-breaths take twice the time of in-breaths. Research has shown that practicing this type of breathing keeps the airways of people with asthma more open than before they started practicing yoga and less likely to tighten up when irritated. A study in Australia in 2002, for example, compared the lung functions and asthma symptoms of a group of asthma sufferers who practice yoga with a group that do not. This study found a significant reduction in asthma symptoms in the group that practiced yoga. Other studies have found that yoga breathing also regulates levels of oxygen and carbon dioxide in the bloodstream, counteracting the effects of hyperventilation. According to research scientist and yoga expert Robin Monro, "Yoga can be very valuable to asthmatics. One reason is that it teaches breathing with movement, and asthmatics are often very tense around

Yoga involves breathing techniques that can improve an asthmatic's ability to breathe.

the chest and diaphragm, very locked in their breathing. Yoga can teach asthmatics to relax and open up the diaphragm, so that they can learn to use it properly."[32]

Another way to improve breathing is the Buteyko method, developed by Konstantin Buteyko, a Russian doctor who theorized that asthma is caused by hyperventilation. The Buteyko method teaches asthmatics to change their breathing patterns in order to alter the balance of carbon dioxide and oxygen in their bodies. Patients learn to breathe through their nose, rather than their mouth, and to suppress the urge to gasp for air. This is accomplished by consciously pausing between inhaling and exhaling. Courses in the Buteyko method take five days and are led by specially trained teachers. Buteyko method teachers report that 85 percent of the patients who learn the Buteyko method reduce their use of short-term reliever medication, and 75 percent have fewer asthma attacks. According to one asthma sufferer who practices the Buteyko method, "During the five days I was doing the course I noticed that I had no symptoms of asthma, so I was able to reduce my dependency on the reliever medication and six months down the track I was able to reduce the preventer medicines without any recurrence of the asthma."[33]

Loosening Chest Muscles and Strengthening the Rib Cage

Alternative treatments that seek to loosen chest muscles and strengthen the rib cage include chiropractic care and acupuncture. Since frequent asthma attacks can lead to a barrel-chested, hunched-over posture, which tightens the chest muscles and makes deep breathing difficult, one of the goals of these treatments is to improve asthmatics' posture in order to loosen the chest muscles and make breathing easier.

Chiropractic care focuses on reaching this goal by manipulating the spine of asthma patients. According to chiropractic theory, an asthmatic posture leads to misalignment of the spine, which through the spinal cord and nervous system is linked to and affects the lungs and airways. This misalignment is thought to result in breathing problems. So, manipulating the spine and properly straightening it will lead to decrease in asthma symptoms. Performed by licensed health professionals called chiropractors, chiropractic treatment involves applying gentle force to the spine to remove pressure, loosen stiff areas, and allow healthy breathing patterns to occur naturally.

Although the effectiveness of chiropractic theory has not yet been proven, many asthma patients find relief through chiropractic therapy. In fact, chiropractic treatment has become such a popular form of alternative treatment that the National Institutes of Health is currently studying its effects on the body. An asthma patient describes how chiropractic treatment has helped her: "I am asthmatic and routinely go to a chiropractor. I have found that I breathe more easily after an adjustment. It does not cure my asthma, but it does help make me more comfortable."[34]

Acupuncture is another treatment that loosens chest muscles and strengthens the rib cage. Acupuncture is an ancient form of Chinese medicine based on the theory that healthy people have a life energy called chi flowing through their bodies; if this energy flow becomes blocked, illness occurs. Acupuncture involves the insertion of hair-thin needles into specific points in the body where acupuncturists believe energy channels are blocked. The needles are thought to stimulate the flow of energy through these points. Once the flow of energy is restored, acupuncturists believe that the immune system will function better. This results in a reduction in lung hyperresponsiveness, decreased mucus production, relaxed airways, loosened chest muscles, and improved posture.

A number of studies have found that acupuncture does relax both the airways and chest muscles. Western scientists theorize that acupuncture needles affect the nervous system, which controls muscles around the chest and airways. Acupuncture causes the muscles in the airways to relax and makes breathing easier for asthmatics. In addition, acupuncture seems to make patients feel more relaxed and to improve general health. According to one asthma sufferer, "I had asthma quite badly. My doctor wasn't doing anything except prescribing more and more Ventolin. A friend suggested I see an acupuncturist. So I did, and my asthma started clearing up. It was incredible."[35]

Consequently, many doctors recommend acupuncture as a complementary treatment for asthma. In a survey done in Europe in 1999, 25 percent of family doctors agreed that acupuncture is helpful for asthma patients. In fact, acupuncture has become so popular as a complementary treatment that a growing number of medical doctors also train as acupuncturists.

During acupuncture, needles are inserted into various parts of the body. Acupuncture can help asthma patients breathe better by relaxing their muscles and opening their airways.

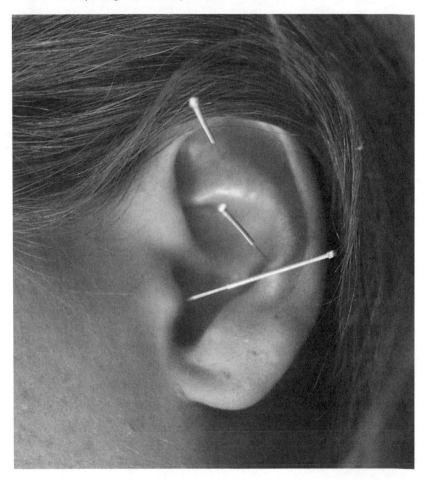

Controversial Methods

As a result of the large number of people who want to reduce their dependence on asthma medicine, a thriving industry offering alternative treatments for asthma has developed. Many of these treatments, such as acupuncture and meditation, have a long history of use and effectiveness and appear to offer patients relief. But the effectiveness and safety of other treatments that have not been tested or used widely are more controversial. Among the most controversial treatment methods are those that claim that, because they are derived from natural ingredients, they are safe. This, however, is not always the case. If a natural substance is strong enough to treat an illness, it is also strong enough to negatively affect a person's health.

Herbal treatments are one such controversial method. Herbal treatments are a commonly accepted alternative treatment for a wide range of diseases, such as bladder infections, digestion problems, and arthritis. But because of the number of asthma patients who suffer from allergies, herbal treatments can be dangerous when used by asthmatics. Herbal treatment, which uses leaves, stems, seeds, and roots of plants known to have healing properties, is based on the theory that when certain herbs are ingested, they can reduce inflammation, strengthen the immune system, and control or eliminate asthma symptoms. In certain illnesses, such as arthritis and hepatitis, some herbs do reduce inflammation, but they often do the opposite when used by people with asthma.

Other complications often arise due to the lack of regulations of herbal products. Unlike the monitoring of conventional medicine, in which government agencies supervise the level of active ingredients, levels of active ingredients in herbs are not monitored, and there are no set dosage levels. Thus, the herbs may be too strong. There have been cases in which the strength of herbal products has been found to be three times the amount stated on the label. This can lead to a bad reaction. For example, high doses of popular herbs used to treat asthma, such as lobelia, licorice, and ephedra, can cause high blood pressure, dizziness,

Herbal remedies can be dangerous if used by asthmatics.

liver injury, heart problems, and even death. Accordingly, Dr. Renata Engler, chief of allergy immunology at Walter Reed Medical Center, warns, "It is important to remember that the use of complementary medicine [particularly the use of herbs] constitutes a type of self-experimentation and carries unknown risk for the individual."[36]

Other controversial treatment methods are products that promise to eliminate asthma symptoms. Some of these products, such as sprays that claim to permanently remove allergens caused by pet hair, are ineffective. This is because such claims are simply untrue. Even when patients remove pets from their homes, for example, microscopic bits of pet hair remain for a number of years. Scientists have not yet discovered a way to eliminate these allergens.

In other cases, devices used to treat asthma can make a patient's asthma worse. For example, air ionizers and vaporizers, which also claim to clean the air in the homes of asthmatics, are often used to remove asthma triggers and relieve asthma symptoms. However, these products are not just ineffective but can actually make asthma attacks more severe. Ionizers and vaporizers increase humidity in the air, which can lead to an increase in mold and dust mites, two common asthma triggers.

Alternative diagnostic tests can also be controversial. One such test claims to identify allergens that trigger asthma by analyzing hair samples. In this test, a sample of a patient's hair is sent to a laboratory, where analysts examine and measure the mineral content in the patient's hair. Believers in hair analysis think that the mineral content in a person's hair is linked to specific allergies, which can be treated with mineral supplements. There is no proof that analyzing hair samples can identify allergens, however, or that treatment with mineral supplements can keep asthmatics from reacting to allergens. Even so, many people with asthma do undergo this test in an effort to avoid uncomfortable skin-prick allergy tests.

How Safe Are Alternative Treatments?

Controversial or not, many patients are turning to alternative treatments hoping to find gentler and more effective therapies for asthma. However, alternative treatment, like conventional treatments, can pose serious health risks. One of the greatest risks occurs when people replace conventional treatment with alternative treatment. Alternative treatments may improve asthma symptoms temporarily, but they do not improve lung function or clear an asthmatic's airways once an attack is in progress. Thus, relinquishing conventional treatment completely can be extremely dangerous. Without quick-relief medicine, for instance, a mild asthma attack can quickly escalate

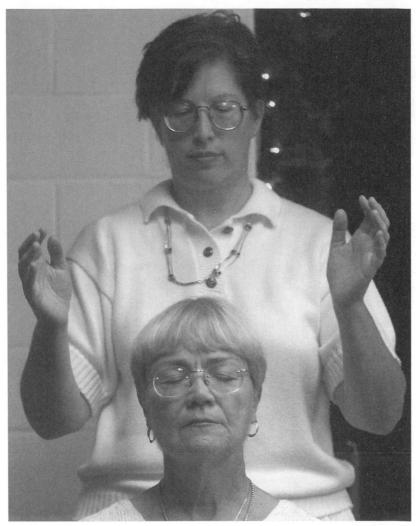

A practitioner (standing) assists a patient with an alternative treatment. Such treatments can be successful when combined with conventional medicine.

into a life-threatening situation. A young man who had this experience explains:

> After I finished the Buteyko breathing course, I was overconfident. I thought, who needs medicine, when you know how to breathe correctly? Besides, I'd been swimming every day, and that made me feel stronger. Between the swimming and the

Buteyko course, I thought I was Superman. I stopped taking everything. I didn't even bother to carry my inhaler with me. I didn't tell my doctor, either. I figured he wouldn't approve. That was so stupid. Asthma is a dangerous disease, but I had to learn the hard way. I wound up in the emergency room sucking down oxygen through a nebulizer [a special type of inhaler that converts liquid to gas]. It was scary. I'll never be that foolish again.[37]

The lack of mandatory licensing of many alternative practitioners can also present health risks. Even seemingly harmless alternative treatments such as yoga can be damaging when led by an instructor who lacks experience in working with asthmatics. This is because it is possible to do yoga breathing incorrectly, and if this practice is not corrected, the result is sometimes hyperventilation.

Aromatherapy oils (pictured) emit strong odors and can often trigger asthma attacks.

Even treatments performed by certified practitioners can pose health risks. Chiropractic treatment is one such treatment that can sometimes be damaging. Overly vigorous manipulation of the spine can cause serious injury. This is especially true in young children whose bones are thin and fragile. Some asthma patients report spinal fractures and pinched nerves as a result of bad chiropractic treatment.

Aromatherapy can also produce difficulties for asthmatics. The scented oils used in aromatherapy can sometimes cause problems since strong smells can trigger asthma attacks. Tests on asthma patients have shown that there is a direct link between the nose and the airways. Substances inhaled through the nose can irritate the airways and cause them to contract. Although the irritation and resulting problems in the airways may be mild in some people with asthma, it may result in a life-threatening attack in others.

Despite the dangers that alternative treatments can pose, many people with asthma successfully combine alternative treatments with medication. When used properly, such a combination can reduce patients' dependence on asthma medicines, lessen long-term health risks, and make asthmatics feel more in control of their lives. As an asthma patient who successfully combines alternative treatment with asthma medicine explains, "Combining the two has helped me feel better physically and emotionally. I feel like I know how to help myself. Rather than being completely dependent on medicine, I'm in control."[38]

Chapter 4

Living with Asthma

L IVING WITH ASTHMA is not easy. People with asthma face many challenges. However, by taking steps to keep their symptoms under control, most people with asthma lead active and happy lives.

What Is It Like to Live with Asthma?

People with asthma face the threat of an asthma attack occurring at any time. This often results in feelings of stress, anxiety, and fear. Consequently, many asthma patients feel as if they have lost control of their lives and that their asthma is controlling them. To eliminate the persistent threat of an asthma attack, people with asthma adopt a number of measures to help manage the disorder. These measures often include making changes in their lives that lessen asthma symptoms. According to one asthma sufferer,

> My asthma was pretty bad all the time, and it just dominated my life, it stopped me doing so many things. I felt I really couldn't go on like that. It wasn't any sort of life. Now I feel like I've really gotten on top of it, and I hardly ever get asthma attacks. I'm much more careful about avoiding dust and cats, which makes a big difference. Last year I started doing yoga classes. I don't hang around with people who smoke anymore. I just feel so much healthier now. I haven't needed my inhaler for months.[39]

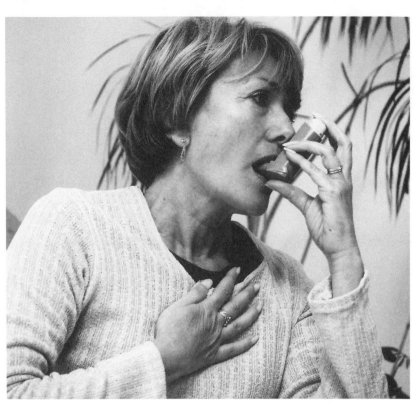

A woman uses an inhaler to control an asthma attack. Asthma attacks can occurr at any time.

Identifying Triggers

One of the first steps people with asthma take to manage their disorder is identifying specific substances that trigger their attacks. The American Lung Association advises asthma patients to "be a detective. Use the clues you have to figure out what causes you to have an attack. If you can figure out what causes an attack, you can stay away from those triggers."[40]

To do this, many people with asthma keep an asthma journal. In an asthma journal, patients record how they feel every day. They note their emotional state, general health, and asthma symptoms. They also include specific details such as what the weather was, what they ate, where they went, who they were with, what activities they participated in, and what, if any, effect these things had on their asthma. Using this information, patients and doctors can analyze what factors encourage or worsen a person's asthma symptoms and pinpoint specific triggers. Once specific triggers are identified, patients can try to avoid them. In this manner, people with asthma gain more control over the disorder.

Managing Triggers at Home

Once specific triggers have been identified, people with asthma often take steps to remove them from their homes. Eliminating common triggers such as dust mites, mold, cockroaches, and animal hair can help prevent asthma attacks.

A dust mite, as seen through an electron microscope. Droppings left by dust mites are a common household asthma trigger.

Dust mites are one of the most common asthma triggers. Dust mites are microscopic spiderlike creatures that live in dust and leave their droppings in carpets, upholstered furniture, bedding, and curtains. Experts estimate that the average bed contains more than 2 million dust mites. Special bed covers that repel dust mites are one way that asthmatics can reduce the number of creatures. Another is using a dehumidifier to dry out household air, since dust mites thrive in moist air. In order to completely dislodge dust mites, however, asthmatics often remove carpets, curtains, and upholstered furniture, replacing them with tile or wood floors, miniblinds, and leather, wood, or vinyl furniture. A woman with asthma who made some of these changes in her home says, "Having found that I was allergic to dust mites, I bought a powerful dehumidifier, anti-mite covers for the bedding, and a marvelous vacuum cleaner. The change that they have made to the quality of my life is enormous. I have never felt better."[41]

Like dust mites, mold also needs humidity to flourish. It often grows in bathrooms, damp basements, garbage cans, refrigerators, and houseplants. Therefore, many people with asthma also use their dehumidifiers to keep mold from growing in their homes. In addition, some people with asthma get rid of houseplants in an effort to minimize their exposure to mold.

Cockroach droppings are another common household asthma trigger. Cockroaches are especially troublesome in apartments where the bugs can move easily through the walls. To eliminate this trigger, asthma patients often hire an exterminator to destroy cockroaches in their home. During the fumigation and for several hours afterward, asthmatics must stay out of their homes, since the chemicals used in the process can irritate their sensitive airways and cause an asthma attack. For this reason, asthmatics wait to return home until the chemical fumes dissipate. As a final step, asthma patients often seal cracks in the walls to keep cockroaches from reentering their homes.

Pets can also trigger asthma attacks. Although pets are beloved members of many households, pet dander, which is made up of pet hair, saliva, and skin, is a common asthma trig-

Pet dander can trigger asthma attacks. Some owners choose to give up their pets to lessen their asthma symptoms.

ger. In fact, pet dander affects about 30 percent of asthma patients. As a result, even though giving up a pet can be very difficult, many people with asthma do this in order to lessen their asthma symptoms. Asthmatics who have pets generally keep their pets outdoors as much as possible. When allowed indoors, the pets tend to live in a restricted area that the asthmatic stays away from. An asthmatic who gave up her pet explains her decision: "Newton was a stray kitten. He was the cutest, sweetest little thing. I adored him. But once he came to live with me, I experienced more frequent asthma attacks. I tried keeping him off the furniture, but it didn't help. It broke my heart, but I had to give him up. The vet helped find him a good home. I miss him, but I don't miss the asthma attacks."[42]

Managing Triggers at School

Managing asthma triggers away from home can be more difficult, and schools pose a special problem. Triggers found in schools include chalk dust; chemicals used in science labs; strong-smelling substances like glue, paint, and markers; or pet dander from classroom pets. And these cannot easily be avoided by asthmatic students. Instead, students and their families must find other ways to cope.

One way asthmatic students cope is by developing a school asthma action plan. This plan includes information from the student's doctor informing teachers, school officials, and the school nurse about the student's asthma, what triggers it, what medications are needed, and what procedure to follow in an emergency. Keeping these people informed helps students with asthma manage their symptoms at school more effectively. For example, teachers may seat asthmatic students away from triggers, and students may be monitored more closely than usual on the playground for symptoms of exercise-induced asthma.

Many schools do not allow students to keep any form of medication, including short-term reliever medicine, with them, so students have to store their inhalers in the nurse's office. However, with an asthma action plan on file, school officials often permit students with asthma to keep their inhalers with them, allowing the students to respond quickly to an attack. A student with asthma talks about how important this can be:

When I first started having asthma attacks, I had to go to the nurse's office to get my inhaler. I had to run downstairs, feeling all short of breath and wheezy. Sometimes, even if I couldn't breathe, I had to wait in line behind kids getting their temperature taken or throwing up. It felt like forever before I could get my inhaler. That only made the attacks worse. So, I had my doctor send a note to school. Now I'm allowed to carry my inhaler with me, and my teachers are fine with it. I use it whenever something triggers my asthma. Because I can get to my inhaler whenever I need it, I rarely have a serious attack.[43]

Avoiding Cigarette Smoke

Despite the best efforts, it is not possible to eliminate all asthma triggers. Thus, people with asthma also often choose not to participate in certain activities in order to avoid triggers. One activity asthamatics rarely take part in is smoking.

Secondhand smoke can cause asthma and other respiratory problems.

Many people with asthma who smoke quit, and those who do not smoke usually avoid people who smoke and social events in smoky environments.

Smoking, which damages the lungs of people without asthma, is particularly dangerous to the weak and sensitive lungs of asthmatics. Smoking makes asthma worse and can lead to the development of other lung diseases such as emphysema, a serious respiratory disease. Breathing secondhand smoke is also a problem. It can cause wheezing, the development of respiratory infections, decreased lung function, and more frequent asthma attacks. Secondhand smoke is particularly damaging to children with asthma. Children's airways are smaller and narrower than an adult's and thus more easily irritated. According to the American Academy of Allergy, Asthma, and Immunology, secondhand smoke worsens asthma symptoms in more than 1 million children with asthma each year.

Because of the danger of secondhand smoke, problems can arise for asthmatics when friends and family members smoke. In order to protect their health, many people with asthma end friendships with smokers and change their leisure activities in an effort to avoid smoky bars, cafés, or restaurants. According to one asthma patient, "If I come in contact with anyone smoking I get this particular type of cough and my lungs lock up. I don't go to smoky venues of any sort, and if people are smoking in a room I leave."[44]

Avoiding Aspirin

Aspirin and other over-the-counter drugs are another dangerous trigger that many people with asthma must avoid. Approximately 10 percent of asthmatics have a very bad reaction to aspirin. It can cause severe, and occasionally fatal, asthma attacks. This is because the sensitive airways of asthmatics are easily irritated by a chemical called acetylsalicylic acid found in aspirin.

There are several hundred other medications, such as ibuprofen found in Advil and Motrin, that contain aspirinlike substances. Many of these are sold over the counter, meaning people can buy them without a doctor's prescription. Therefore, asthmatics must be extremely cautious when taking any medicine. A patient talks about his experience:

> I had a bad cold and I bought some over-the-counter cold medicine to help me get a good night's sleep. Instead, I spent the night in the E.R. [emergency room]. I have to stay away from aspirin. It aggravates my asthma. Turns out the cold medicine had a chemical in it that's just like aspirin. Live and learn. Now I carefully read the labels on any medicine I take. If I don't know if something is similar to aspirin, I ask the pharmacist. It's a bother, but so is a night in the E.R.[45]

Sports Participation

Sometimes people with asthma also have to change the type of sports they participate in. Sports such as track and field that involve prolonged running; those such as ice skating and skiing that are done in cold air; and those such as scuba diving that use thin, pressurized air may trigger asthma attacks. Many asthmatics choose not to participate in these sports, or they take steps to adapt their participation to manage their asthma. One such adaptation is taking a puff of short-term reliever medicine fifteen minutes before participating in sports. This relaxes and opens up the airways and keeps them open for about three hours. This protects athletes while strenuous exercise is taking place. Warming up before exercise is another way athletes with asthma help decrease the chance of an asthma attack. Warming up reduces the likelihood of the airways tightening by warming the air in the lungs. Finally, another change many asthmatics make is wearing protective clothes while participating in sports. For example, by covering their mouths and throats with a warm scarf while skiing or skating, people with asthma keep cold air from entering their airways. This prevents the airways from contracting and aggravating asthma symptoms.

Most asthmatic athletes know their limitations and stop exercising when symptoms threaten. They also restrict activity when they have a cold or infection. By making these kinds of adaptations, many people with asthma have become successful athletes. Olympic swimming gold-medal winner Nancy Hogshead explains the adaptations she has made:

> I stop swimming workouts immediately whenever I feel that I've reached a point where my asthma is coming on. It always pays to be aware of your asthma status. If you feel your asthma is particularly aggravated by colds and flus, then ease up a bit on your exercise program if you have the sniffles, body aches, or feel particularly run-down. You might even consider eliminating a workout or two until you feel completely better. There is nothing wimpish about this. A world-class athlete pushes his or her body in one sense, but knows how to baby it as well.[46]

Professional athlete and Olympian Nancy Hogshead suffers from asthma. Many asthmatic athletes adapt their participation in sports to manage their symptoms.

Monitoring and Maintenance

People with asthma face the threat of an asthma attack occurring at any time. Thus, to manage their asthma and prevent attacks from occurring, they must regulate their condition and take whatever steps are needed to maintain open airways. As a result, many people with asthma take long-term controller medication every day and carry an inhaler with short-term reliever medicine at all times. In addition, many patients use a machine called a nebulizer at home. A nebulizer is an air compressor that discharges an easy-to-inhale mist of asthma medication into asthma patients' airways. A patient describes a nebulizer: "I use my inhaler when I'm not at home. But when I'm home, I use a big machine called a nebulizer that you plug in to the wall. You put liquid medicine into it and you wear a mask. It turns the liquid into a gas and you breathe the gas in. It's much easier to get air into my lungs with the nebulizer. If I feel like I'm having an attack, I get on the machine. I can even use it while I watch TV."[47]

Another way people with asthma manage asthma symptoms is by monitoring their breathing. Often, asthmatics feel like their breathing is fine when it is not. This is because many asthmatics do not have noticeable asthma symptoms when their airways first begin to narrow. By using a small, easy-to-use machine called a peak flow meter, which measures the amount of air patients expel from their airways, people with asthma can monitor changes in their airways and be alerted to a possible asthma attack.

When patients blow into the peak flow meter, an indicator moves to one of three color zones (green, yellow, or red) that are designated by the numbers 0 through 100. A reading in the green zone falls between 80 and 100 and indicates good lung functions. A reading between 50 and 80 falls in the yellow zone. This warns patients to take quick-relief medicine because asthma symptoms appear to be worsening. Consistent yellow readings indicate that patients need stronger or more frequent long-term controller medication. A reading below 50 falls in the red zone, signaling danger and the start of a severe asthma attack. When this occurs, patients immediately take quick-relief medicine and seek medical help.

By using a peak flow meter, patients learn to recognize symptoms leading up to an asthma attack, and take steps to prevent the attack from occurring. According to Barbara Weintraub, a critical care nurse who works with many asthma patients, "Peak flow results are an indicator of asthma severity. Typically the peak flow will start to drop prior to the onset [before the start] of the sensation of either breathlessness or wheezing. Therefore, daily monitoring of peak flows for chronic asthmatics could prompt them to initiate [begin] the next step of treatment [before an attack starts]."[48]

Managing allergies is another way asthmatics control their asthma. Asthmatics who are allergic to a number of things frequently take weekly allergy injections in order to reduce the effect of allergy-related asthma triggers. Allergy injections, or desensitizing therapy, consist of diluted doses of pollens and other triggers that patients have tested positive for during allergy skin testing. Repeated injections with allergens build up in the patient's body until the immune system no longer feels threatened by them. This desensitizes the immune system, making it less likely to overreact to allergy-induced asthma triggers. An asthma patient talks about her experience: "I'm extremely allergic to a number of different plants. Just being around them aggravates my asthma. I've tried several different medicines, but when the pollen count goes up, nothing helps. My doctor suggested I try allergy shots. I was wary because I hate needles. But I hardly feel it. They use small, fine needles. Best of all, my asthma problems have diminished."[49]

Since respiratory infections can worsen asthma symptoms and cause a prolonged decrease in lung functions in the sensitive lungs of asthma patients, taking steps to avoid infection is another way people with asthma help control the disorder. Research has shown that germs that cause coughs, colds, and the flu also cause an abnormal immune response in asthmatics. This results in extremely high levels of inflammation, leading to severe

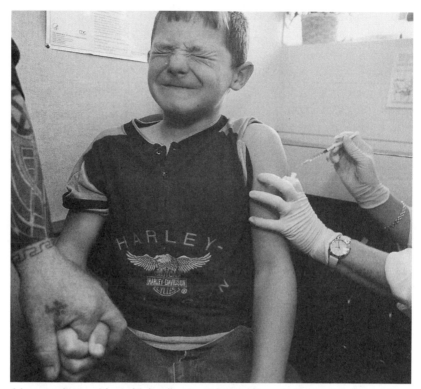

Many patients with multiple allergies take injections to lessen the effects of asthma triggers.

asthma attacks. Experts are unsure why this occurs, but they advise people with asthma to get an annual flu vaccine in order to lessen their risk of contracting the flu and developing dangerous asthma symptoms.

Becoming Self-Aware

Another important step people with asthma take is becoming self-aware. This involves patients learning all they can about asthma. Becoming knowledgeable about their disorder helps asthmatics become better able to recognize the symptoms that precede an attack. Consequently, they can take necessary precautions to reduce those symptoms and prevent or minimize the severity of an attack. When patients do not have this awareness, they often ignore asthma symptoms. This can escalate into a life-threatening situation. According to a boarding school principal who works with, and is responsible for, many students with asthma, "The people who die are not those who are known to be serious asthma sufferers. Those people [the serious asthma sufferers] know themselves very well, they've seen the limits, they've experienced the danger and they are very good at monitoring themselves and getting attention quickly and properly. The people who have died don't notice the asthma attack coming on, and all of a sudden they're in trouble."[50]

One way asthmatics can become self-aware is by participating in an asthma support group. Asthma support groups are made up of people with asthma who share their experiences. These groups give members a chance to express their feelings and provide information, encouragement, and a sense of belonging. By sharing their common experiences, support group members often find solutions to problems that nonasthmatics do not understand. A woman with asthma who attends a support group explains how it has helped her: "It's good to know there are other people like me. We share our problems, talk about our medications, laugh at ourselves, and provide each other with the kind of support and understanding that our friends without asthma can't provide. I would recommend that everyone get involved in a support group. Because of this group, I feel stronger. I've learned more about asthma and how to live with it."[51]

There are asthma support groups all over the country for asthma patients of all ages, including special groups for adults, children, and teens. Organizations such as the American Lung Association and the Asthma and Allergy Foundation of America sponsor local support groups in towns and cities throughout the United States. For example, groups meet regularly in Fort Worth, Texas; Albuquerque, New Mexico; Tucson, Arizona; and Queens, New York. In addition, there are electronic support groups that share information via the Internet.

Asthma Camps

Many children and young adults with asthma also develop self-awareness and asthma management skills by spending their

Children with asthma can go to special camps to learn how to manage asthma symptoms.

summers attending special camps for juvenile asthma patients. These camps are sponsored by the American Lung Association in conjunction with the Consortium on Children's Asthma Camps. By teaching asthmatics how to recognize and manage symptoms, asthma camps help juvenile patients learn ways to meet the challenges they face every day. For example, with the help of counselors and other campers, asthmatics develop plans to avoid asthma triggers; they also receive instructions and practice in using their inhalers correctly. The camps also give children with asthma a chance to participate in physical activities like softball, archery, boating, and swimming that accommodate their limitations. All of the activities are supervised by a special medical staff that provides assistance in case anyone has an asthma attack. According to one young man with asthma, "I went to asthma camp, and it was lots of fun. They give you breathing tips, and they do lots of physical exercises, not jumping jacks or push-ups but physical games that are fun and strengthen your lungs. We talked about problems we have with asthma and learned some solutions. There were lots of interesting kids there, and I met new friends."[52]

The asthma management skills and self-awareness that patients gain in support groups and asthma camps help asthmatics manage their disorder. When this is combined with careful monitoring and lifestyle changes, people with asthma gain control over their symptoms. This allows them to live happy, active, and productive lives.

Chapter 5

What the Future Holds

ALTHOUGH EXPERTS KNOW how to help people with asthma manage asthma symptoms, they cannot fully explain what factors cause asthma to develop. If these factors could be identified, scientists could use this knowledge to prevent the development of asthma. A number of current research studies are exploring the causes of asthma.

Identifying the causes of asthma could help some patients soon, but its greatest impact will be on future patients. Thus, scientists are also working on the development of safer and more effective treatments. Such treatments would help all people with asthma right now.

Blame It on Modern Life

Because the number of asthma cases has almost doubled in the last twenty years, and continued growth is predicted, scientists are centering their research on investigating the factors specific to modern life that encourage the development of asthma. According to Dr. Jonathan Brostoff,

> The asthma epidemic is affecting all the rich, Westernized countries of the world. It is also affecting immigrants to Western countries arriving from places where asthma is rare. For example, when people from the Polynesian island of Tokelau move to New Zealand, their chances of getting asthma double. Similar increases have been seen among Filipinos moving to the U.S.A. and Asians from East Africa

moving to Britain. It is obvious that the asthma epidemic is being caused by some factor or factors in modern Westernized life."[53]

Scientists hope that by identifying these factors and developing effective methods to combat them, they will be able to prevent or lessen the incidence of asthma in the future.

Environmental Factors

To identify what factors have encouraged the recent surge in asthma cases, researchers have tried to determine how modern life differs from life in the past. They theorize that changes in

Researchers believe that air pollution has caused an increase in the number of asthma cases.

society resulting from the growth of industry and the movement of people to urban areas have fueled the increase in asthma rates. This is because, in the past, when most people lived in rural areas with unpolluted air, the incidence of asthma was low.

By comparing the incidence of asthma in modern urban populations to the incidence in more primitive, rural environments, scientists are gaining evidence to support their theory. One study that examined the incidence of asthma among South Africans moving from a rural village to the capital city of Capetown found asthma rates twenty times greater among immigrant families living in Capetown. Another study compared the asthma rates of people living in the formerly divided cities of East and West Berlin. East Berlin, which according to scientists was approximately forty years behind in modern urban conditions (such as the type of air pollution, industrial development, and the type of diet most commonly consumed), had a significantly lower rate of asthma than more modern West Berlin. Evidence from these and other studies has led scientists to accept the validity of the theory that changes in society resulting from industrial growth and the movement of people to urban areas have led to an increase in the incidence of asthma. Consequently, scientists are trying to identify specific factors in modern society that may encourage the development of asthma.

One such factor is air pollution. A study examining the relationship between asthma and air pollution compared the incidence of childhood asthma in West Oakland, California, with childhood asthma rates in the rest of the state. West Oakland was chosen for the study because it has very high levels of air pollution caused by nearby manufacturing plants and diesel-fueled truck traffic. According to the results, children in West Oakland are seven times more likely to be hospitalized for asthma than children in the rest of California.

A similar study looked at asthma rates in Calexico, California, and Mexicali, Mexico, two cities along the California-Mexico border where the air quality is below health standards. Once again, asthma rates in these cities were well above normal. According to Eric Niiler, a journalist who reported on the study,

> There are a number of on-going studies looking into the causes of asthma. But there's no doubt that air pollution makes it worse. The U.S. Environmental Protection Agency says the air [in these cities] violates health standards for carbon monoxide, ozone [smog] and particulate matter [dust and dirt in the air]. The problem extends to Mexicali, where one local doctor who specializes in treating respiratory diseases estimated that 15 percent of the population has asthma. That's twice the normal rate in Mexico.[54]

Specific Pollutants

Because polluted air is composed of a number of different substances, scientists want to pinpoint exactly which pollutants encourage asthma to develop. If specific pollutants can be identified, scientists can focus on developing ways to eliminate these substances from the air, or develop treatments to combat their effects.

Among the substances being examined is ozone, or smog. Smog is created when exhaust fumes from cars and trucks are exposed to sunlight. Scientists already know that ozone constricts the airways of both asthmatics and nonasthmatics and is a common asthma trigger. However, recent evidence has led experts to believe that ozone not only triggers asthma symptoms but also causes asthma to develop. A study in Southern California tracked and compared, for a period of five years, new asthma rates in nonasthmatic children who played organized sports in high-smog and low-smog communities. Athletes were chosen for the study because athletes generally breathe deeply and rapidly, causing them to inhale twenty times more pollutants than nonathletes. And children were chosen because they are more likely to develop asthma than adults. The study found that the children in the high-smog communities were three times more likely to develop asthma than the children in the low-smog communities.

As a result, in order to reduce the development of asthma, organizations such as the National Institute of Environmental Health Science are urging the Environmental Protection Agency to take steps to reduce air pollution, such as requiring that motor vehicles use cleaner fuel. And athletes (both asthmatic and nonasthmatic) are being alerted to limit outdoor activity to about an hour a day when unhealthy air quality is expected. According to researcher Dr. Rob McConnell of the University of Southern California, "This study [in Southern California] has shown that ozone can cause asthma. Reducing levels of ozone is the ideal solution. But even limiting prolonged outdoor activity of children when air pollution levels are high could help."[55]

Dangerous Gases

Other studies have investigated the effects of gases like diesel exhaust fumes, produced by motor vehicles, and nitrogen dioxide and sulfur dioxide, produced by factories. All three are known to be asthma triggers. Studies into whether sulfur dioxide and diesel exhaust fumes aid the development of asthma are inconclusive, but nitrogen dioxide appears to encourage asthma to develop. A Canadian study compared asthma development in children exposed to either high or low levels of nitrogen dioxide to children who were not exposed to the chemical. The study found that the subjects exposed to low levels of nitrogen dioxide were two-and-a-half times more likely to develop asthma and those exposed to high levels of nitrogen dioxide were ten times more likely to develop asthma than the subjects who were not exposed to the chemical at all.

Scientists are connecting these studies to the sudden development of asthma among rescue workers at the 2001 World Trade Center disaster. Many rescue workers who rushed to save victims from the collapsing buildings failed to wear special masks that screen out harmful pollutants, known as respirators. As a result, the workers' airways were exposed to harmful gases such as nitrogen dioxide and benzene, along with dust composed of finely ground concrete, glass, smoke, and chemicals. Shortly thereafter, more than seven hundred

Some September 11th rescue workers developed "World Trade Center cough" from inhaling dangerous gases.

rescue workers reported developing asthma symptoms. A fire-fighter who developed asthma symptoms, including a disturbing cough referred to as the "World Trade Center cough," describes his experience: "In the morning [the cough is] heavy. It feels like a powder on the back of your throat. You can't take a deep breath sometimes."[56]

The existence of sudden asthma symptoms among World Trade Center rescue workers has given scientists the opportunity to study the effects of nitrogen dioxide and other gases, and to study how asthma responds to early treatment. To encourage these studies, the Centers for Disease Control gave New York City $5 million to conduct research. As a result, a number of ongoing studies are under way. One study is examining the relationship between the severity of breathing problems and exposure to specific pollutants. Another is attempting to determine how effective respirators are in screening out pollutants and stopping the development of asthma by comparing the lung function of workers who used respirators with those who did not. Still another study is attempting to determine whether early treatment can stop asthma from developing into a chronic problem by comparing the difference in asthma symptoms in workers who received asthma treatment within the first three months of exposure to pollutants and those who did not. Scientists hope that the results of these studies will protect people exposed to dangerous levels of pollutants from developing asthma in the future. Dr. Stephen Levin, the medical director of the Mount Sinai Hospital Center for Occupational and Environmental Medicine, explains: "Studies of people exposed to the [World Trade Center] disaster might show whether early treatment with inhaled steroids really does lower the risk that newly diagnosed asthma will become a lifelong condition."[57]

Indoor Pollution

Another area of investigation is the effect of indoor pollution on the development of asthma. The National Institute of Environmental Health Services is sponsoring an ongoing study known as the Environmental Intervention in the Primary Prevention of Asthma in Children (EIPPAC). This study is investigating the theory that reducing exposure to indoor pollutants such as dust mites and cockroaches will decrease the incidence of asthma. The study is based on evidence from other studies showing that exposure to dust mites and cockroaches increases people's chances

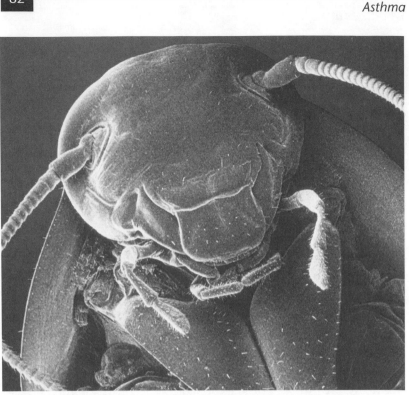

Exposure to insects such as cockroaches (above) can increase people's chances of developing asthma.

of developing asthma. Researchers in the EIPPAC study are collecting and analyzing indoor pollution samples gathered in inner-city apartments in Boston and checking lung functions and asthma rates of the residents. Researchers selected inner-city apartments in Boston for the study because indoor pollution and high asthma rates are problems for inner-city dwellers, whose homes are usually older, more moldy, and have more insects than other apartments. Scientists hope the study in Boston will shed some light on indoor asthma triggers.

On the basis of the study's results, scientists will analyze the effectiveness of different ways to combat dust mites and cockroaches. These include sealing cracks in the walls, setting roach traps, installing special indoor air cleaners and dehumidifiers, and encasing bedding in special dust-mite-resistant covers. Scientists theorize that reducing inner-city residents' contact with dust mites and cockroaches will lower the prevalence of asthma. EIPPAC researchers anticipate that "information obtained from this study will lead to [ways to avoid and eliminate triggers] that will positively impact the respiratory health of Americans, particularly children in low income, inner-city households."[58]

Diet

While some scientists are looking outside the body for factors that encourage the development of asthma, others are looking within the body at the role diet plays. Many scientists speculate that, since the middle of the twentieth century, the rise in the use of preservatives, the popularity of fast foods rich in salt and fat, and the decrease in the consumption of fruits and vegetables are linked to the increase in the incidence of asthma. Consequently, a number of studies during the past ten years are examining these links. Two European studies, for example, compared the incidence of asthma in people who eat fruit with those who do not. Both studies found that the subjects who eat the most fruit are the least likely to develop asthma.

Other studies examined the link between vitamin C, a vitamin found in many fruits, and the prevention of asthma. Evidence shows that there is a lower incidence of asthma in people who consume large amounts of vitamin C, compared to those with low levels of the vitamin in their bloodstream. Scientists theorize that since vitamin C is an antioxidant, a substance that helps the body fight disease and poisons, it helps prevent asthma by counteracting the effect that dangerous substances, such as smoke and pollutants, have on the lungs. In addition, studies have found that vitamin C has anti-inflammatory properties, which helps keep the airways from constricting and mucus from forming. As a result of the evidence gathered in these studies, experts encourage people with a family history of asthma to eat fruits rich in vitamin C, such as oranges, pineapples, and grapefruit. According to Dr. Jonathan Brostoff, "Children from families with a tendency to allergy and asthma may benefit enormously from a diet of this kind: it could make the difference between developing asthma and staying healthy."[59]

Another nutrient, magnesium, a mineral found in green vegetables, is also believed to discourage the development of asthma. A study in England that compared the lung functions of people who ate foods containing large and small quantities of magnesium found that the subjects who ate the most magnesium had the healthiest airways. Scientists hypothesize that an unidentified chemical in magnesium helps relax muscles, thus keeping the airways open and reducing the development of asthma. As a result, scientists are urging everyone to eat more green vegetables. The magnesium in the vegetables may, scientists believe, prevent people from getting asthma.

Harmful Nutrients

Just as certain nutrients may help prevent a person from getting asthma, other nutrients appear to encourage its development. This is particularly true for salt. A study in Kenya compared nonasthmatic children with a high-salt diet to those with a low-salt diet. The study's results showed that children on the high-salt diet were 60 percent more likely to develop asthma than those on the low-salt diet. Although scientists are unsure why salt is harmful to the airways, they theorize that some property of salt directly affects the muscles surrounding the airways, causing them to contract.

Scientists are also investigating several ingredients common in fast foods because these foods generally contain high levels of fat and preservatives. Oil and fat, for instance, seem to lead to an increased risk of developing asthma. Scientists do not know why this is so and are continuing to investigate. In addition, sulfites, a common preservative found in prepared and fast foods, seem to affect the development of asthma. Sulfites are powerful asthma triggers in some people. They contain a chemical that can irritate the airways and cause severe asthma attacks. Ongoing studies are trying to determine whether sulfites may also encourage the development of asthma in people with sensitive lungs.

Even though scientists have not found conclusive evidence that salt, oil, fats, and sulfites can cause asthma, it appears that eating a healthy diet can reduce asthma symptoms and the sever-

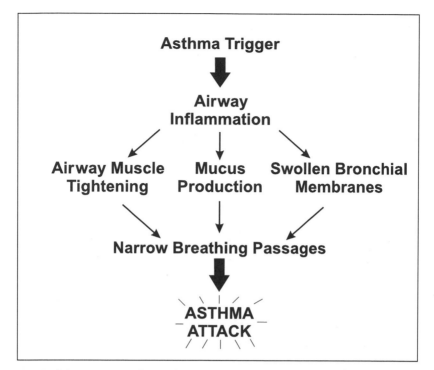

ity and frequency of attacks. Consequently, many asthma experts suggest that people with a family history of asthma eat foods that seem to prevent asthma and avoid those that seem to encourage its development. Dietitian Amanda Ursell explains: "While inhalers and steroids remain the drugs of choice to treat asthma attacks, . . . taking nutritional steps may help reduce the number of asthma attacks experienced in the first place."[60]

Genetic Factors

Other scientists are looking even deeper into the body at the role genes play in the development of asthma. Genes are tiny cells found in every living thing that determine individual traits such as hair color, eye color, and height. There is mounting evidence that genetic factors put people at a greater risk of developing asthma. Because genes are passed down from parents to children, scientists have been analyzing families in the United States, Australia, and Europe, seeking conclusive evidence of the genetic transmission of asthma among family members. These studies have found that genetic factors did encourage the development of asthma in two-thirds of the subjects studied. Moreover, researchers found that identical twins, who share exactly the same genes, were more likely to develop asthma than nonidentical twins, and exhibited the same asthma symptoms with the same level of severity. According to researcher Dr. Eugene R. Bleeker, "Recent findings suggest that genes may not only reflect a risk of the development of asthma, but also modulate disease severity [determine how severe asthma is] once it has developed. Better understanding of the genetic mechanisms that contribute to asthma may lead to identification of individuals at high risk and potentially customized [adapted and individualized] treatment regimes."[61]

A scientist examines lung tissue samples in a laboratory. Many scientists believe that asthma may be transmitted genetically.

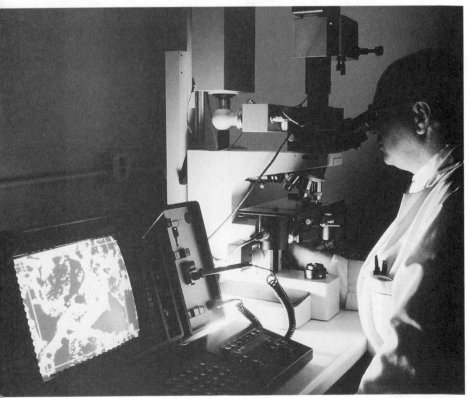

As a result of these studies, researchers are trying to identify specific genes found in all asthma patients. If such genes are identified, scientists hope to develop a way to replace or modify them in order to prevent or treat asthma. Scientists throughout the world are conducting multiple studies to pinpoint asthma genes. One study analyzed DNA samples of three hundred people living on Tristan da Cunha, an island in the South Atlantic where 30 percent of the population has asthma. A specific mutated gene was found in all of the subjects with asthma but not in the nonasthmatics. A similar study in England gathered DNA samples from three hundred families of asthma sufferers and found a defective gene in 40 percent of all the subjects with asthma. As a result of studies like these, scientists have so far identified about thirty genes that they believe are associated with asthma.

Scientists speculate that, since these genes are found only in asthmatics, they may actually cause asthma to develop. Consequently, ongoing research is investigating the effect these genes have on the body. As knowledge about how these genes affect the body increases, scientists hope to develop a method to pinpoint the genes in affected people and take measures to prevent or delay the onset of asthma.

Finding New Treatments

Scientists hope that investigating the genetic factors that encourage the development of asthma will help prevent it in the future. However, they are also working on developing new and more effective treatments to help asthma patients now. Much of this research involves the use of computer technology. Researchers in California have created a computer model of virtual asthma patients on which they test different treatments. Each virtual patient has a different severity of asthma, from mild intermittent to severe persistent. This way, researchers can determine how a variety of patients respond to different drugs. Using this computer-based technology, scientists can replicate and complete research in weeks that might take years in a standard laboratory. So, new medication can reach the public more quickly than in the past.

One of the drugs being tested is an anti-inflammatory medication called anti-IgE. This drug stops the action of an antibody or protein known as immunoglobin E (IgE). IgE is produced in everyone. However, people with asthma appear to produce larger than normal quantities of IgE. Scientists believe that the overproduction of IgE is the primary cause of allergic reactions in asthma. When an allergen enters the lungs, white blood cells carrying IgE travel to the airways to attack the allergen. Anti-IgE attaches to these white blood cells and produces a chemical that removes IgE from the cells. Without IgE, the white blood cells are powerless to attack the allergens, inflammation is blocked, and an allergic reaction in the airways of asthma patients is prevented. Tests have shown that anti-IgE greatly reduces the amount of IgE in white blood cells and lessens the severity of the airways' response to allergens. According to a report by William W. Busse in *Discover* magazine, "Anti-IgE may make it possible to remove one of the most important keys to allergic reactions, and consequently, lessen the severity of asthma."[62]

Other studies are testing a new type of inhaler. This inhaler, called a discus inhaler, helps asthmatics keep track of when they take their medicine. It also helps prevent patients from accidentally taking in too much medicine. The discus inhaler is round and is equipped with a counter on one side that makes a clicking sound when a prescribed dose of medicine has been inhaled. The click alerts patients that further inhalation will result in an overdose, and the counter helps patients track their remaining doses. For example, if patients are required to take a dose of medicine daily for thirty days, the counter begins at thirty and decreases by one number each time a patient takes the correct dose of medication. A patient who tested the inhaler as part of a clinical study describes his experience:

> I used it for a study for eight months. It was so easy to use. Right when you hear it click, you know you breathed in enough. With regular inhalers, sometimes you wind up gagging and coughing after you take a puff because you took in too much. With this, you know when to stop. It also helped

me to keep track, because I get off track and forget whether I took a dose or not. This new inhaler makes having asthma a lot easier.[63]

With many ongoing studies into the causes of asthma, and the development of new, more effective, and easier-to-use treatments, the future looks bright for people with asthma. A cure may be found in the future, but for now, new treatments give asthmatics hope.

Notes

Introduction: A Growing Epidemic

1. Quoted in Jonathan Brostoff and Linda Gamlin, *Asthma: The Complete Guide to Integrative Therapies.* Rochester, VT: Healing Arts Press, 2000, p. 95.

2. Daniel, interview with the author, Dallas, TX, March 7, 2002.

3. Daniel, interview with the author.

Chapter 1: What Is Asthma?

4. Quoted in Kathryn Shafer and Fran Greenfield, *Asthma Free in 21 Days.* San Francisco: Harper San Francisco, 2000, p. 14.

5. Betty B. Wray, *Taking Charge of Asthma.* New York: John Wiley & Sons, 1998, p. 2.

6. Brostoff and Gamlin, *Asthma,* p. 22.

7. Bryan, interview with the author, Dallas, TX, March 8, 2002.

8. Quoted in Brostoff and Gamlin, *Asthma,* p. 126.

9. Quoted in Brostoff and Gamlin, *Asthma,* p. 236.

10. Andrew, interview with the author, Dallas, TX, March 7, 2002.

11. Monica, interview with the author, Dallas, TX, March 25, 2002.

12. Sarah, interview with the author, Dallas, TX, March 1, 2002.

13. Wray, *Taking Charge of Asthma,* p. 1.

14. Andrew, interview with the author.

15. Bryan, interview with the author.

16. Quoted in Brostoff and Gamlin, *Asthma,* p. 62.

Chapter 2: Diagnosis and Conventional Treatment

17. Quoted in Brostoff and Gamlin, *Asthma*, p. 220.

18. Quoted in Susan Fitzgerald, "Asthma Often Goes Undiagnosed in Young Athletes," *Philadelphia Inquirer*, November 30, 2001.

19. Teddy, interview with the author, Dallas, TX, March 26, 2002.

20. Quoted in Alt.Support.Asthma, "How Is Asthma Diagnosed?" www.radix.net.

21. Quoted in Allergy and Asthma Network—Mothers of Asthmatics, "Noisy and Quiet Medication." www.aanma.org.

22. Monica, interview with the author.

23. Quoted in Asthma Reality, "My Story." http://asthmereality.com.

24. Quoted in About.Asthma, "Parent's Corner: What Is Considered Long-Term Treatment?" http://forums.about.com.

25. Daniel, interview with the author.

26. Quoted in Brostoff and Gamlin, *Asthma*, p. 333.

Chapter 3: Alternative and Complementary Treatment Strategies

27. Teddy, interview with the author.

28. Quoted in Brostoff and Gamlin, *Asthma*, p. 297.

29. Monica, interview with the author.

30. Margaret Hutchby, Hypnosis for Health and Happiness, "Pain and Physical Conditions." www.hypnosis4therapy.co.uk.

31. Teddy, interview with the author.

32. Quoted in Brostoff and Gamlin, *Asthma*, p. 399.

33. Quoted in Catalyst, "Asthma: An Alternative Treatment." www.abc.net.au.

34. Quoted in About.Asthma, "Complementary Remedies: Chiropractics." http://forums.about.com.

35. Quoted in Brostoff and Gamlin, *Asthma*, p. 412.

36. Quoted in Wray, *Taking Charge of Asthma*, p. 143.

37. Daniel, interview with the author.

38. Teddy, interview with the author.

Chapter 4: Living with Asthma

39. Quoted in Brostoff and Gamlin, *Asthma*, p. 1.

40. American Lung Association, "Teens and Asthma: What You Really Need to Know." www.lungusa.org.

41. Quoted in Brostoff and Gamlin, *Asthma*, p. 141.

42. Monica, interview with the author.

43. Bryan, interview with the author.

44. Quoted in Brostoff and Gamlin, *Asthma*, p. 203.

45. Daniel, interview with the author.

46. Quoted in Wray, *Taking Charge of Asthma*, p. 127.

47. Bryan, interview with the author.

48. Quoted in *RN*, "A Helpful Guide to Asthma Education," September 2001, p. 28.

49. Cindy, interview with the author, Dallas, TX, April 3, 2002.

50. Quoted in Brostoff and Gamlin, *Asthma*, p. 63.

51. Cindy, interview with the author.

52. Bryan, interview with the author.

Chapter 5: What the Future Holds

53. Brostoff and Gamlin, *Asthma*, p. 79.

54. Quoted in Melissa Block, "Analysis: High Rates of Asthma Among Populations Living Close to the California-Mexico Border," *All Things Considered* (NPR), January 17, 2002.

55. Quoted in MSNBC News, "Air Pollution Linked to Asthma." www.msnbc.com.

56. Quoted in Malcolm Ritter, "Response to Terror: Ground-Zero Workers Air Concerns Over Health Impact," *Los Angeles Times,* January 13, 2002.

57. Quoted in Ritter, "Response to Terror."

58. Asthma Research at NIEHS, "Primary Prevention of Asthma: The EIPPAC Study." www.niehs.nih.gov.

59. Brostoff and Gamlin, *Asthma*, p. 97.

60. Amanda Ursell, "On Nutrition: How Diet Plays a Role in Asthma Attacks," *Los Angeles Times*, March 18, 2002.

61. Quoted in Allergy and Asthma Network—Mothers of Asthmatics, "Genes, Lifestyles, and Microbes Provide New Clues About Allergies and Asthma." www.aanma.org.

62. William W. Busse, "New Approaches to the Treatment of Asthma," *Discover*, March 1999, p. 25.

63. Andrew, interview with the author.

Glossary

adrenaline: A powerful chemical that the body produces naturally when it is threatened or excited; it allows the body to react to an emergency by raising blood pressure and heart rate and opening up breathing passages.

airways: A roadlike network in the body through which air travels in and out.

allergens: Harmless substances, such as pollen or dust, that the body reacts to inappropriately.

allergy: An overreaction by the immune system to allergens.

alternative treatment: Nontraditional medical treatments.

antibody: A special protein found in the immune system that attacks foreign invaders.

anti-inflammatory: A drug used to block inflammation.

antioxidant: A substance that helps the body fight disease and poisons.

asthma: A disorder of the respiratory system that affects the lungs and the ability to breathe.

asthmatic: A person with asthma.

beta agonist: A commonly used quick-relief medicine for asthma.

beta-receptors: Cells located in the small muscles surrounding the airways.

bronchi: Two small tubes that connect to the lungs.

bronchioles: Small tubes in the lungs where oxygen is exchanged for carbon dioxide.

bronchodilator: Medication used to open up the airways when an asthma attack threatens.

chronic disorder: A disorder with no foreseeable end.

corticosteroids: Drugs used to control inflammation.

cromolyn: A drug used to control inflammation and the production of histamines.

dander: Pet hair and skin.

dust mite: A microscopic insect found in dust that can trigger asthma.

histamine: A chemical produced by the immune system to fight allergens.

hyperreactive lungs: The lungs of people with asthma that over-react to things in the airways that do not normally trouble other people.

hypnotherapy: An alternative treatment in which patients are put into a trance to learn to relax.

immune system: The system that protects the body from foreign invaders.

immunoglobin E: An antibody involved in allergic reactions.

inflammation: The body's best defense against germs, characterized by swelling, redness, and the production of mucus.

inhaler: A device that allows medicine to be inhaled directly into the airways.

irritant: A substance that causes the airways to become inflamed.

isocyanate: A chemical found in spray paint, rubber, and plastic that is extremely irritating to the lungs.

long-term controllers: Drugs taken over a long period to control inflammation in asthma.

meditation: An alternative treatment in which patients calm their minds.

mucus: A thick gooey substance produced by the respiratory system to trap irritants.

nebulizer: A special type of inhaler that converts liquid medicine into a fine mist.

peak flow meter: A device that measures lung functions.

phlegm: A form of mucus.

pollen: A powder produced by plants that can trigger asthma.

quick-relief medicines: Drugs used to open up the airways when an asthma attack threatens.

respiratory system: The body system that controls breathing.

smog: Air pollution caused when chemicals produced by cars and trucks are exposed to sunlight.

spirometer: A device used by doctors to measure lung functions when patients inhale and exhale.

status asthmaticus: A life-threatening asthma attack.

sulfur dioxide: A chemical produced by some factories that triggers asthma.

theophylline: A drug used to control inflammation in asthmatics.

trigger: A substance that provokes an asthma attack.

wheezing: A whistling sound made when the airways are constricted.

windpipe: A long, hollow tube through which air travels from the nose or mouth to the lungs.

Organizations to Contact

Allergy and Asthma Network—Mothers of Asthmatics
2751 Prosperity Ave., Suite 150
Fairfax, VA 22031
(800) 878-4403
www.aanma.org

The Allergy and Asthma Network offers information about asthma in children and young adults, including lists of doctors who treat asthma, the latest asthma news, and an information hot line.

American Academy of Allergy, Asthma, and Immunology
611 Wells St.
Milwaukee, WI 53202-3889
(800) 822-2762

www.aaaai.org

This organization provides information on allergies and asthma. It offers pollen and pollution reports throughout the United States, a twenty-four-hour hot line, and free educational materials.

American Lung Association
1740 Broadway
New York, NY 10019-4374
(800) 586-4872

www.lungusa.org

The American Lung Association provides information on every aspect of asthma. It discusses and supports new research and sponsors local support groups.

Asthma and Allergy Foundation of America

1125 15th St NW, Suite 502
Washington, DC 20005
(800) 7-ASTHMA

www.aafa.org

This organization provides educational material, newsletters, an asthma information line that operates twenty-four hours a day, and lists of local support groups.

National Center for Complementary and Alternative Medicine

Clearinghouse
PO Box 8218
Silver Springs, MD 20907-8218
(888) 644-6226

http://altmed.od.nih.gov

This organization conducts research on the effectiveness of alternative treatments and provides information on a wide variety of alternative treatments.

For Further Reading

Books

William E. Berger, *Allergies and Asthma for Dummies*. Foster City, CA: IDG Books Worldwide, 2000. This book gives a wealth of information about allergies and asthma in an easy-to-read format.

Susan Dudley Gold, *Asthma*. Berkeley Heights, NJ: Enslow, 2000. A simple book that discusses what asthma is, what an attack is like, and how it is treated.

Alvin Silverstein, Virginia Silverstein, and Laura Silverstein Nunn, *Asthma*. Berkeley Heights, NJ: Enslow, 1997. This young adult book examines every aspect of asthma, including its history and its effect on society.

Carolyn Simpson, *Everything You Need to Know About Asthma*. New York: Rosen Publishing Group, 1998. This book examines what asthma is, its treatment, and what it is like to live with the disorder.

Peggy Guthart Strauss, *Relieve the Squeeze*. New York: Viking, 2000. A book with bright colors and lots of photographs that discusses how to control asthma in an interesting fashion.

Websites

Children's Medical Center, University of Virginia (www.med.virginia. edu). This site offers simple interactive lessons on asthma and the respiratory system for children and young adults.

Draw a Breath Educational Program (www.drawabreath.com). This site is dedicated to educating the public about asthma. It also provides information about asthma summer camps and swim programs.

Works Consulted

Books

Jonathan Brostoff and Linda Gamlin, *Asthma: The Complete Guide to Integrative Therapies.* Rochester, VT: Healing Arts Press, 2000. Looks at causes, diagnosis, treatment, and ways to cope with asthma.

Phil Lieberman, *Understanding Asthma.* Jackson, MS: University Press of Mississippi, 1999. Presents information on all aspects of asthma, including causes, treatment, and care.

Kathryn Shafer and Fran Greenfield, *Asthma Free in 21 Days.* San Francisco: Harper San Francisco, 2000. Discusses the effects of asthma on the body and alternative treatments.

Betty B. Wray, *Taking Charge of Asthma.* New York: John Wiley & Sons, 1998. Discusses asthma causes and treatments as well as numerous tips on managing the disorder.

Periodicals

Melissa Block, "Analysis: High Rates of Asthma Among Populations Living Close to the California-Mexico Border." *All Things Considered* (NPR), January 17, 2002.

William W. Busse, "New Approaches to the Treatment of Asthma." *Discover*, March 1999.

Susan Fitzgerald, "Asthma Often Goes Undiagnosed in Young Athletes," *Philadelphia Inquirer*, November 30, 2001.

Matt Ridley, "Asthma, Environment, and the Genome." *Natural History*, March 2000.

Malcolm Ritter, "Response to Terror: Ground-Zero Workers Air Concerns Over Health Impact." *Los Angeles Times*, January 13, 2002.

RN, "A Helpful Guide to Asthma Education." September 2001.

Amanda Ursell, "On Nutrition: How Diet Plays a Role in Asthma Attacks." *Los Angeles Times*, March 18, 2002.

Internet Sources

About.Asthma, "Complementary Remedies: Chiropractics." http://forums.about.com.

———, "Parent's Corner: What Is Considered Long-Term Treatment?" http://forums.about.com.

Allergy and Asthma Network—Mothers of Asthmatics, "Genes, Lifestyle, and Microbes Provide New Clues About Allergies and Asthma." www.aanma.org.

———, "Noisy and Quiet Medication." www.aanma.org.

Alt.Support.Asthma, "How Is Asthma Diagnosed?" www.radix.net.

American Lung Association, "Teens and Asthma: What You Really Need to Know." www.lungusa.org.

American Lung Association of Minnesota, "The Consortium on Children's Asthma Camps." www.alamn.org.

Asthma Reality. http://asthme-reality.com.

Asthma Research at NIEHS, "Primary Prevention of Asthma: The EIPPAC Study." www.niehs.nih.gov.

Catalyst, "Asthma: An Alternative Treatment." www.abc.net.au.

Margaret Hutchby, Hypnosis for Health and Happiness, "Pain and Physical Conditions." www.hypnosis4therapy.co.uk.

MSNBC News, "Air Pollution Linked to Asthma." www.msnbc.com.

Index

acetylsalicylic acid, 66
acid reflux, 26
acupuncture, 44, 50, 51–52
adrenaline, 24–25, 38
African Americans, 22
air pollution, 77–78
allergens, 12, 16
    see also chemicals;
        cockroaches; dust
        mites; mold; triggers
allergies, 12–13, 29–30, 53,
    70–71
allergy tests, 29–30
American Academy of
    Allergy, Asthma and
    Immunology, 66
American Lung
    Association, 60, 72, 73
animal hair. See pet
    dander
antibodies, 88
anti-IgE, 88
anti-inflammatory
    medicines, 88
    see also corticosteroids
antioxidant, 83

anxiety, 59
aromatherapy, 47–48, 58
aspirin, 66–67
asthma
    African Americans and,
        22
    allergens and, 12, 16
    allergies and, 12–13,
        29–30
    alternative treatments
        for, 43–58
    athletes and, 18–29
    breathing habits and,
        40–42
    chemicals and, 16
    children and, 28
    costs of, 10
    coughing and, 14
    damage from, 23–24
    definition of, 8
    description of, 12,
        15–16
    devices for management
        of, 69–70
    diagnosis of, 26–31, 55
    diet and, 83–85

Picture Credits

Cover Photo: © David K. Crow/PhotoEdit/Picture Quest
© AP/Corpus Christie Caller-Times, 56
© AP/Northeast Miss Daily Journal, 54
© AP/Ocala Star Banner/Bruce Ackerman, 57
© Associated Press, AP, 17, 20, 41, 47, 49, 68, 71, 80
© Lester V. Bergman/CORBIS, 30
© COREL Corporation, 63, 76
© Ecoscene/CORBIS, 10
Alan Iglesias, 13, 14, 85
© James Marshall/CORBIS, 73
© PhotoDisc, 9, 18, 40, 45, 51, 86
© Photoresearchers, 23, 27, 32, 34, 60, 61, 66, 82
© Ted Spiegel/CORBIS, 37
USDA, 17

About the Author

Barbara Sheen has been a writer and educator for more than thirty years. She writes in both English and Spanish. Her fiction and nonfiction books have been published in the United States and Europe. She currently lives in Texas with her family, where she enjoys weight training, swimming, reading, cooking, and animals. This is her fourth book in Lucent's Diseases and Disorders series.